CONFESSIONS OF A SPANISH TEACHER

Vicki Marie Riley

CONFESSIONS OF A SPANISH TEACHER

Vicki Marie Riley

For Mum, Dad, Tony, Elaine, and Terry.

I miss you all.

See you on the other side.

CONFESSIONS OF A SPANISH TEACHER

Vicki Marie Riley

INTRODUCTION

It has been so difficult to start this book...

Simply because of not knowing where to start.

Whenever you try to think of where a story starts- that is the hardest.

Life is a series of events and decisions, each one leading to the next.

Every event and the decision we take consequently takes us one way or another, and we can never know what would have happened had we taken the other fork in the road.

As much as we may mull things over and wonder, we will never know.

That´s why Soren Kierkegaard famously said-

"Life can only be understood backwards, but it must be lived forwards".

Another favourite quote of mine is Omar Khayyam:

"The moving finger writes and having written moves on. Nor all thy piety nor all thy wit, can cancel half a line of it."

Maybe one day when we cross over to the other side our sliding doors moments will be shown to us.

This book is called "Confessions of a Spanish Teacher", so I suppose I should start with how I became one.

Where did my Spanish journey start?

No idea.

People quite often ask –

"Why did you come to Spain?"

I feel like replying, do you have a couple of weeks to spare while I tell you?

It is the hardest thing to condense into just one reason.

Did it start when I was just a little girl and I used to tell my dad that one day I would live abroad?

I have no idea where I got that idea from as my family were the least adventurous family travel-wise that you could imagine.

We NEVER went abroad, both for financial reasons and the fact that my dad hated flying and any kind of foreign food. He had seen enough during the war. He was a typical working-class Mancunian of his day, child of Irish immigrants.

In his Navy days he had travelled to places like Dubai, but he was of a generation that had a general distrust of anything foreign. This improved as he got older somewhat, but he never came to Spain to visit.

In fact, I remember him saying "they are all savages there you know" when I said I was coming here to live, and asked ridiculous questions like "do they have bins over there? ".

My dad was a product of his time, he did not know any foreign people in his youth. As I say, he did get better as he got older, maybe helped by my own gravitation towards foreign people and a brief marriage to a man from Hong Kong, whom he adored. I think my mother and father were more devastated than me when we separated.

My Mum was more adventurous, she would go anywhere and do anything, and my Dad was quite happy to let her go off with her friends. So maybe that´s where my gypsy nature came from.

Unfortunately, by the time I came to Spain she was suffering from various illnesses including dementia and she never got here either.

I have decided to start this story from just before I went to live in Reading, my first step on experiencing a different kind of life.

Also, the events that transpired there in my life were the catalyst that propelled me inexorably to Spain.

If you believe in such things, as I do, I was destined to come here. Every event that transpires in your life is a lesson, where you take it and how you deal with it is the reason for your existence.

I feel I have had an "interesting" life so far, and when I say that I am not bragging.

A Chinese curse says,

- "May you live in interesting times".

Interesting is not always good. I quite envy people who are happy to stay in one place and not feel the restlessness that has plagued me all my life.

I have friends from my youth who still live in the same house and even still have the same telephone number. Part of me envies that and part of me knows it would never have suited me.

I feel I sacrificed financial security and relationships with family and friends for new experiences.

I don´t know if this was the right thing to do, it just felt like the right thing to do at the time.

I hope you find my story interesting. I will try to be as honest as possible without causing hurt or offence to anyone.

My goal is to make you cry with me at least once, be angry with me at least once, and to laugh with me many times.

Thank you for reading this.

CONFESSIONS OF A SPANISH TEACHER

Vicki Marie Riley

CHAPTER ONE- THE BEGINNING

19 is a difficult age for all generations

However. each distinct generation has unique problems.

For my parent´s generation really it was the Second World War that defined them.

They had to grow up quickly as many of them fought and died for their country.

Homosexuality was illegal, mental health was considered an illness to be ashamed of.

Racism was not talked about simply because often this generation had not even met anyone of a different ethnic group.

Women had their place, but it was less than a man´s place.

I cannot really comprehend this as I did not experience this.

Today´s nineteen-year-olds have been defined by the Covid Pandemic, mental health awareness, climate change, gender freedom, racial equality and social media.

They are free to choose their gender and sexuality and even celebrate it, and racism of course still exists but it is generally frowned upon and at least discussed.

However, the weight of the world´s problems is upon them through their telephones and television screens.

If they don´t die of suicide or Covid 19, climate change will get them.

I cannot comprehend much of this either, but I welcome it.

I do feel we have moved on as a society, though we still have a long way to go.

When I was 19, some things were better, some things were worse.

It wasn´t that no one had mental health issues, I know from family experiences many people certainly did.

However, you certainly didn´t discuss it with anyone, least of all your parents. To be gay was still difficult to admit to anyone and the advent of the Aids virus made that situation even worse.

The HIV information on the television was so terrifying, that when a student told me a couple of years ago that he is HIV positive I am ashamed to say that my first reaction was horror.

Those stark advertisements worked so well all those years ago. Anyone of my age group will remember the tombstone adverts and the general opinion that HIV was a death sentence.

It was only a momentary reaction, almost involuntary, that I shook off immediately. High-profile people such as Princess Diana helped to dispel that myth. I remember so clearly when she hugged the HIV positive children in the hospital without fear and with so much love.

Luckily, this prejudice gradually faded, and we know the truth about Aids now.

Although our generation (I believe they call us Generation X) was not at war like that of my parents, the ongoing Cold War with Russia did have us more or less certain that a nuclear war could break out at any moment.

Adverts told us to get under the table in such a situation.

Yes, that would save us.

I clearly remember being literally terrified that this war might happen.

However, there were many positive things about the world that we lived in.

Jobs were easy to find, and education was free.

At 17 I had left college and gone to work full time at Lewis´s Department Store in Manchester City Centre.

I didn´t want to study any more, most of my friends were working and I just wanted to earn money and go out partying.

In those days' parents, certainly in the working-class world I came from- did not support their children after 16 years old. You were expected to work, and jobs were abundant, so it was easy to do so. I was told in no uncertain terms that I would have to pay my way.

I earned 25 pounds a week at Lewis´s. I thought I was rich.

5 pounds went to my parents for my “keep”- (though it was normally borrowed back before the next pay day)

20 pounds went on alcohol mostly and clothes etc.

A good night out could be had on a fiver-

4 Cherry B´s or Babychams for a pound, a pound for the last bus home, a couple of pounds entry into the club, and the rest of the evening seeing how many boys you could get to buy you a drink.

Life was a continuous party and I just lived for my next night out and boys, boys, boys.

I also worked a couple of nights at the weekend in a bar next to the department store, the Trafalgar, for extra money for more nights out.

I remember on a Sunday I would lie in bed until 2 o’clock, exhausted from work and fun.

My feet would be throbbing after so long standing on them and I would literally get up at about 2pm just to eat the roast dinner my Mum had prepared and be back in bed not that long afterwards.

Good times and thank God there was no social media to embarrass you forever.

My poor parents. How great it would be to be able to do that now, no worries about bills or responsibility, just relentless fun, and no cleaning, cooking, or washing up.

Shame we don´t appreciate it at the time.

I often consider myself lucky to still be alive after so many drunken nights and lifts home accepted from more or less anyone, even if they had been drinking.

How I never got murdered or killed in an accident I will never know.

My journey of life was meant to continue.

At 19, I managed to become a clerical officer for the Civil Service.

My Dad was overjoyed- "A job for life, love".

I lasted 2 years and nearly died of boredom. Hats off to anyone who sticks out a job like that until they get their pension, normally early. They bloody deserve it.

However, in that short time a couple of things happened that changed my life forever.

As I mentioned- that time for me was a time for partying and fun.

Now I was earning better money than at Lewis´s and was out practically every night.

I have always had lots of friends and one of my best friends at the time was a girl called Elaine. Elaine lived just around the corner from me and worked in the City Centre in an office.

She had this brilliant job, I thought at the time. I was so envious.

She could choose her own hours provided the work got done.

She was a night bird, and she would lie in bed until late and go to work in the afternoon, coming home in the evening.

These days I am a definite morning person, but I wasn´t then, so I was so jealous that she could lie in bed all morning and choose what time she went to work.

She lived with her mum and was the absolute centre of her mum's life. Her dad had left years before and he now had a new family.

I cannot remember how we met. It was either through a mutual friend or on a night out.

Although she lived relatively close to me we had not known each other in childhood.

She had been with a long-time boyfriend, but they had recently separated, so we started to go out together in search of boys.

She did find another boyfriend quite soon, but as far as I remember we still carried on going out.

Elaine was a very beautiful girl. Slim, blue eyes, petite.

She had the most gorgeous blonde hair in a kind of "Farrah Fawcett" style which was so popular at the time from the TV programme "Charlie´s Angels"

Shortly before the incident I am about to relate she had this hair cut shoulder length for some unknown reason, but to this day whenever I think of her it is with long hair not short.

It was coming up to Christmas, and both Elaine and I were buzzing.

We loved Christmas, as did any teenage girl.

It was a time for presents, parties, dressing up and having time off work.

What more could a young girl want.

Elaine was particularly excited as she was looking forward to her work Christmas party.

She worked for a Law Firm, and they always went to really nice places for their Christmas parties. This was so unlike the Civil Service (my employment at the time), where the party was always held at the DHSS office in Rusholme near Moss Side.

This was of course not so glamorous, but it was bloody good fun anyway. I could probably write a book just about those escapades.

I was the make-up expert, and she was going to come around to my house on the day of the party, so that I could do her hair and makeup.

In the lead up to Christmas it was all that she talked about, she could not wait.

The day of the party approached.

It was approximately 2 weeks before Christmas day itself, though I do not remember exact dates.

That fateful night I had gone to bed quite early, around 9 o´clock.

I know that I was working the next day so it must have been a weeknight.

Around nine-thirty, or possibly earlier, I was dozing off and heard the telephone ring.

Of course, we had no mobiles then.

The truth was, that in our house, we had only had a landline for a couple of years. Before that it was a case of a 15-minute walk to the nearest phone box.

I was in that twilight world between sleep and awake. I heard the telephone ring and was vaguely aware that my Dad answered it, but wasn´t sure if I was dreaming or not.

I distantly heard him say "She´s in bed", and I tried to shout that I was still awake but the words just wouldn´t come out. It was a very strange feeling.

He had hung up the phone before I finally managed to get any words out.

"Who was that?"- I called

"The police"- was the reply (my Dad was a man of few words)

"What did they want?"

"Elaine's mum´s phone number".

All my skin raised in goosebumps, and I felt myself sliding into a kind of twilight zone. My stomach lurched over-I just knew something was badly wrong.

"Why?"

"I don´t know, they wouldn´t say".

"Why can´t she give them her phone number herself and where have they got my number from?"

My dad, who normally had the answer to everything, did not have the answer to that.

Needless to say, it was impossible to sleep after that.

I got up and came downstairs full of more questions that my Dad actually didn´t know the answer to and did not really want to speculate about.

My parents came from that era that didn´t like drama and tried to avoid it at all costs. I suppose that they had had enough drama in the war to last them a lifetime.

My Dad had not even really pressed for information from the policeman, nor asked what station he was calling from- nothing.

My mum had gone to bed already.

I was distraught, I just knew something was terribly wrong.

Fortunately, I did not have to agonise for long. About 5 minutes later the telephone rang again.

It was the police calling back.

They told me that there had been an accident and Elaine had been taken to the hospital.

They had now managed to get hold of her mum and she was on her way there too.

When they asked her mum who if she had anyone that could be with her, she had asked for me. Would I be able to go? They would send a police car for me to take me to the local hospital to sit with her.

I tried to ask them what had happened, but they would not give any information over the phone.

15 minutes later I was dressed, the police car had arrived, and it was taking me to the local hospital. During the journey I tried to ask the policeman what happened. He told me they'd been an accident and Elaine had been run over.

One thing I will always remember is that when I asked how she was, he would only say one thing.

- “She's poorly, she's quite poorly”

That was the extent of the information that the policeman would give me. Now when I look back, I can see why. It was frustrating at the time, but I do understand now with hindsight. He would not have wanted to give any information as that is for the doctor to do I suppose.

Throughout the journey I was imagining seeing Elaine and how we were going to laugh about this. How I would tell her how handsome the policeman was. I had visions of her sitting up in bed with a plaster cast on her leg or arm, or even a whole body in plaster cast, but throughout that car journey it never even occurred to me that she might not recover from this accident.

I only had mental pictures of visiting her in hospital and us eventually having a good laugh about the night that the police phoned. You know, an anecdote to tell through the years of our friendship as our friendship continued, something that we would talk about one day with affection and humour.

A shared experience for two best friends for life. One that was traumatic at the time but that would have a happy outcome.

We arrived at the hospital and her mum was so pleased to see me. As you can imagine she was absolutely devastated. Elaine was the centre of her world, the absolute centre of her world. I comforted her as well as I could.

A nurse came out to speak to us. I know she was trying to comfort us but really it was wrong what she did. When we asked how Elaine was, she said-

"Oh well, she's opening her eyes and she's looking around, so you know that's a positive sign".

We felt a rush of positivity and we thought:

“-Yes, you know she's going to be OK. “

The euphoria was short-lived.

15 minutes later the doctor himself came out, the specialist.

He sat down next to us and told us that Elaine had very severe head injuries and pressure on the brain. They were going to have to operate to relieve this pressure, and that in his experience people who had been operated on under similar circumstances did not recover from this operation.

This was just like a slap in the face after the nurse had told us that she been looking around and that this was a positive sign. All our hope was ripped away in an instant.

It turned out that Elaine was crossing a busy road at traffic lights at a notorious black spot near her home. As a result of this accident the road was completely changed, there were a lot of safety measures implemented.

Unfortunately, it had taken Elaine's accident to make the authorities realise that something needed to be done at this notorious location.

She had been crossing the Princess Parkway at the traffic lights. She had got off her bus after working late as usual, at about 8 p.m.

It was especially tragic as in fact her boyfriend Gary was supposed to pick her up after work, but they had argued over some stupid little thing on the telephone. Either she had either told him not to bother or he had told her to make her own way home.

I think you can probably imagine how that made him feel.

So, Elaine got the bus home.

How the tiny choices we make in life have huge consequences.

Poor Elaine must have been distracted and tried to beat the lights as she crossed over the Princess Parkway to her home. She was minutes away.

She totally misjudged and a car slammed into her and dragged her several yards down the road.

At the subsequent inquest it was found to not be the driver's fault in any way, shape or form. It seems like Elaine just run out in front of him. He wasn't speeding, he wasn't going through a red light, and he was not drunk.

I think probably what happened was that Elaine was still thinking about the argument and did not concentrate properly on the road, though we will never know exactly what happened. I cannot believe that she ran out in front of the car on purpose- though I suppose that was considered at the inquest too. The verdict was accidental death.

The crossing was an accident black spot, Elaine was not the first casualty there unfortunately.

It fell to me to ring her boyfriend Gary with the news.

I just remember how distraught he was when he arrived. It took him about 10 minutes to travel what should have been a half hour journey to the hospital. He was there so quickly it is a miracle that wonder he did not kill anybody else on his way there.

He was as you can imagine heartbroken and felt responsible for what happened, because he should have given her lift home that night.

Then Elaine´s dad appeared and so that was all difficult because her mum and dad were not speaking. They had not spoken for years since they had separated, there was so much bad blood between them. He had married again and had a young family. Her brother Stewart had also arrived, and he occupied himself with Elaine´s father while I comforted her mother.

Elaine went into surgery to relieve the pressure on her brain. I remember I stayed there quite a long time; we were in a waiting room with another family with a loved one in a similar condition after a motorcycle accident.

We got to know that family so well, it was like being in a bubble where only they and us existed. We talked, we laughed, we cried for what seemed hours but today I cannot remember anything about them. I only remember that at some point the surgeon came in to tell them that the operation on their son had been a success and he would recover.

They would soon be able to speak to him. Our feelings were a weird combination of joy and relief for them, combined with a tiny bit of jealousy or envy that their loved one had pulled through. Would we get the same result?

Unfortunately, we would not be so lucky.

From here my recollection is a little bit hazy.

I think we were told that she was out of surgery, which had gone as well as could be expected, and Elaine was now on a life support machine. Only time would tell if her brain would recover from the terrible trauma it had received. We were advised to go home as there was nothing more we could do. Only family would be allowed in to see her.

I simply don't remember if I got a taxi home or whether the police dropped me off. The next day was a normal working day, and my parents told me to ring in sick as I had not slept at all.

However, the thought of just sitting at home thinking was unbearable so off I went to work.

I expect a lot of you reading this have suffered a similar experience of worrying over a loved one's well-being, and we all deal with it in different ways.

I could not just sit around. I was working at the Department of Health and Social Security at the time and that day I was on reception. As you can imagine, we do get quite a lot of very difficult people coming through as well as genuine cases.

I just felt like screaming – "**Don't you know what's happened to my friend?"**

You wonder why the world hasn't stopped turning don't you? But it just carries on, everything carries on as normal. Meanwhile your life will never be the same again.

Elaine was in intensive care on a life support machine for around two weeks. Finally, on Christmas Day the decision was taken by her parents on the advice of the Doctors to turn off the life support machine.

Elaine had been declared brain dead, also the physical injuries to her body were catastrophic. Her pelvis was shattered and nearly every bone was broken. All Elaine ever wanted was to get married and have children- this was never to be for her.

Her mother and father had to make the final awful decision to give permission to turn off the life support machine. That must have been heart wrenching.

You can imagine that from then on Christmas Day was a terrible day for me.

Bereavement is bad enough any time of year, but when you lose someone at Christmas or any other significant date it is even worse. Christmas is rammed down your throat, you cannot escape it or pretend it is not happening. Everyone is celebrating and being with friends and family. Christmas can be excruciating for many people for many reasons.

It was like this for me for many years. For a very, very long time I never ever enjoyed Christmas again. I just could not look forward to it because I thought I wouldn't see it.

Elaine had looked forward so much to that Christmas, and she did not live to see her Christmas party. An enduring memory I have is when the nurse gave us her possessions that awful night, one item was a brand-new dress coat in a boutique bag that she had obviously bought that day for her party.

It was covered in yoghurt that had burst out of a pot that must have been in the bag with it when she was dragged down the road. That sight is still with me as vivid as ever, and even as I write this, tears are falling.

She would have been so happy earlier that day, buying her coat and counting the days until the party she would never attend.

It simply spoiled Christmas obviously for many, many years for me. Christmas had always been a time that I really loved.

I was young, but everyone else was enjoying themselves and talking about Christmas plans etc. As I said, it is always awful to lose a loved one, but even worse having to look at everybody else apparently having a great time while your terrible anniversary is coming up.

Everyone is always asking you what you are doing, etc. and expecting you to join in the festivities.

Eventually. As years passed, I started to think that at least she had the pleasure of enjoying the build-up, if not actually the culmination, and I could not continue refusing to look forward to Christmas just because I might die before it came.

I felt guilty if I did enjoy it, it just did not seem fair that Elaine could never enjoy it again- what right did I have to take pleasure in it?

However, I did not really start to enjoy it again until my son arrived many years later.

Children make Christmas don´t they?

Elaine was a Catholic- so she was buried. Leading up to the funeral I had so many nightmares about my best friend being eaten by worms. Attending her funeral was distressing not only because of this but because of the Priest.

Apparently, Elaine was in purgatory because the last rites were not given, and she would have to atone for her sins before passing on to Heaven.

I was outraged, Elaine was a gentle soul who had never done any harm to anyone.

That awful man offered no words of comfort and just turned his back on Elaine´s mother at the graveside. No embrace, no sympathy offered.

This was the beginning of my antipathy toward the Catholic religion and nothing I have seen or heard of since has changed this opinion.

To me it is simply foul- led by the Vatican- a place of such splendour and riches whilst around the world Catholics starve and live in misery. If you are reading this and are a Catholic, my anger is not directed at you, I respect everyone´s beliefs. However, the institution of Catholicism I detest.

CHAPTER 2- FIRST LOVE

This horrible loss led to another very important event in my life.

Life really is like ripples in a pond, isn´t it- each experience leads to the next and when you look back you can wonder if somehow it is all programmed to happen for whatever mystical reason.

On the 3rd of January following Elaine´s death I was clearly still heartbroken for losing my best friend at such a young age. Another good friend of mine had had a terrible Christmas and New Year for a different reason, as she had split up from her long-term boyfriend.

She was heartbroken as well.

We decided to go out to cheer ourselves up.

We met in town (Manchester Centre) and went to a club called "Cellar Vie" which was a discotheque in the middle of town.

It was a weekday, a Wednesday I believe; it was not a day that we would normally go out.

We were both just so depressed we decided to try and have some fun.

It was freezing cold if not yet snowing, though I know it was certainly snowing the next day because of something else that happened.

Off we went to this discotheque just the two of us and when we first went in there it was practically only the two of us in there. Then we saw a group of lads in the corner.

There were different ethnicities in this group of boys which you know probably now might not seem that strange but then it was quite strange to see such a mix of ethnicities altogether.

I am going back 40 years.

It was maybe not unheard of, but certainly just not the norm.

One boy caught my eye.

He was very tall and very handsome, dressed very nicely. He was Asian, I presumed Chinese but later it transpired he was from Hong Kong.

Christine and I were literally sobbing into our drinks at the bar as “Let’s Stay Together” by Tina Turner was playing.

This had made Christine cry and in turn set me off.

However, as we were the only girls in there our mascara running and puffy eyes did not seem to put them off, and they were looking over at us.

The handsome boy was looking at me for ages, but not doing anything about it. I was smiling at him through my tears, you know like you so when you are trying to give someone a come-on, wordlessly saying:

“Yes, I do like you please come over and talk to me”.

This went on for so long that in the end I thought I was mistaken, and he must be looking at the girl behind the bar behind me. Suddenly one of his friends decided to make a move and approached me.

The boy I liked moved like a shot and arrived first, stepped in front of him and garbled:

- “Want to dance?”

I think he just decided that it was now or never.

If he didn't ask me to dance this other boy was going to and I might say yes. When we started dancing, I could see why it had taken him so long to come over - because he was a terrible dancer.

He was completely without rhythm, and he was trying to balance a drink in one hand and a cigarette in the other, and somehow look cool at the same time.

It was a relief when the music finished, and he asked if I wanted a drink.

I found out later he hated dancing. I do not believe that we ever danced together again.

He told me his name was Damien, which of course was not his real name. His real name was Sui Wing Chu, but they all took Western names to make life easier in the UK. He had taken his from the film, “The Omen”. I think this was an omen!!

We spent the evening together and we arranged to meet the next night outside the Club.

I cannot remember why, but the next day I must have been out drinking in the afternoon because I fell asleep on my sister´s sofa. When I woke up, I was already late for our date, and it would take me at least 30 minutes to get into Town.

I got ready quickly, but I so nearly did not go. I

t was freezing and there was snow on the ground. I arrived at our meeting point 2 hours late, I was convinced he would not still be there.

He was there, frozen and chain-smoking.

He had waited all that time for me. How could I not love him then?

This boy/ man turned out to be really the love of my life. There is nothing quite like first love is there?

We got married quite shortly afterwards but it did not work out.

The culture difference was difficult, we lived with my mum and dad which was not ideal, and there were various other significant problems.

One day before we got married, I was waiting for him to meet me at work, and he never turned up. I waited for hours but I could not contact him as there were no mobile phones in those distant days.

I went home to my sister´s where I was living at the time.

He reappeared the next day, but he would not tell me where he had been. It was years later, when his brother returned to Hong King that he finally told me what happened.

I need to mention another couple of things first which became clear with this explanation. One day in our early dating days I was practically living in the flat he shared with his brother. I was ill one day and stayed home while he went to university. I was in bed and the door opened and it was his cousin. I know him only vaguely and he seemed startled to see me there and left immediately.

Another strange thing that happened was at some point I found a letter of his that had come from Strangeways prison. Of course, it was all in Cantonese and I could not understand a bloody word of it.

No "Google Translate" in those days.

He refused to discuss it with me.

All this made me very insecure.

When he finally told me the full story it all made sense.

His cousin had been part of a Triad gang in Manchester Chinatown. Damian had never wanted to work in the Centre because you could not avoid getting involved in some way.

I knew that one night, only about half an hour after we had been eating in a restaurant there, a Triad gang had come in and chopped up and killed members of a rival gang with hatchets as they were eating. Dangerous stuff.

The day he had "stood me up", his cousin had been arrested and a message was given to Damien and his brother to bring a suitcase that was hidden under the bed (the bed I had been sleeping in the day his cousin popped his head around the door) over to the other side of Manchester.

Damien and his brother opened this suitcase and it contained drugs and a gun.

They did not have a car, and they had to take it on two buses over to the other side of Manchester and hand it over to a Triad member. They were terrified they would be caught either by the police or by a rival gang. He did not want to tell me about it at the time as this knowledge would have been dangerous for me.

I don't want to go into the full details of the relationship and what finally ended it, that is maybe for another book.

Basically, the only reason I wanted to really talk about that is that's part of this steppingstone of why I ended up leaving Manchester in the first place.

I often think about him and hope that life was kind to him. Especially after Hong Kong reverted to Chinese rule.

I believe that first love is unique, when you are young and obsessed with each other and anything seems possible. Some people are lucky enough to stay with that person for the rest of their lives, unfortunately for Damien and I it was not to be.

After our relationship faltered, I just could not stand living in Manchester anymore.

After a (very) brief rebound relationship with someone from work I was ready to live somewhere else.

CHAPTER 3- LEAVING MANCHESTER

One thing that had happened while I was with this man Damien my husband, that helped to lead towards living in Reading was that I left the DHSS.

I was so bored with that job.

Also, when I met Damien, he was at university studying Metallurgy.

When we got married, he decided he wanted to work and earn some money and he went to work in a Chinese restaurant in Alderley Edge not far from where we lived (with my parents).

Now of course he was working nights, but I was working days, weekdays. I was never getting a day off in the week, and he was never getting a day off at the weekend which was when I was off work.

Added to the fact that I was totally bored in that job anyway.

The Civil Service may be a job with a lot of benefits, and I would probably be retired by now on a pension, but I was so bored I just could not stand it any longer.

So, I went to work for Ladbrokes Racing in the betting shops because you could work weekends and get a day off in the week. It was only part time as a cashier/ board marker (the days before screens showed the results) so I could have more time with Damien.

That is all I wanted then.

Of course, as time went on, Damien and I separated and there I was still working at Ladbrokes.

I had a brief relationship with someone else that didn´t work out as I mentioned earlier and by then I had decided to train to be a manager.

We were currently in the Thatcher recession.

I trained and passed my assessment.

However, the Thatcher years had punished Manchester severely and employment had become difficult. We had gone from it being so easy to get a job when I was a teenager to being extremely difficult and practically impossible to get a job.

Ladbroke shops were graded, and I was in a grade nine shop which was the lowest shop. To earn more or progress up the levels you had to move up the grades and eventually you would be aiming towards getting into a grade one shop or a Gold Star shop as they called them.

I know a lot of people loved Margaret Thatcher, and I always respect people´s political opinions.

However, with respect, if you had lived through those terrible times in the North, you would understand why people detested her. So much suffering and lives destroyed through unemployment.

I have a grudging respect for her for her work ethic and convictions, but her total callousness and the selfishness she engendered in British people is hard to stomach. For me that was the beginning of the decline of British society and all the values I was once proud of.

Therefore, in Manchester nobody ever left their jobs as there were no others to go to.

Managers started in a grade 9 shop, and they could be there forever.

No one already in a Grade 1 was going to leave that job and go and work anywhere else because there were no other jobs available that paid the same money.

We were in a terrible recession, but it had not hit the South yet, so when I decided that I would quite like to go and try living somewhere I was interested in the South of England, but not London. I did not want to go to another big city. By now I was 25 years old and not so fussed about partying.

My supervisor at the time, Paul, had already been to Reading and done some sort of supply work there.

They always needed extra staff because they could not find managers there- they simply didn't pay enough money. The job situation was quite the opposite as there was only there was only 4% unemployment. Anyone who really wanted a job could find one.

They wouldn't choose a job at Ladbrokes if they had the choice, they did not pay enough money to someone in the South. However, for me coming from the North it was good. We received extra weighting allowance for being in the South and I was also offered subsidised accommodation. A tied flat if you like, above one of the betting shops.

It was a two-bedroom flat, a very nice flat offered to me at very good price and deducted at source from your wages, so you never had to worry about not paying rent. You knew what money you had left to spend- for me it was great.

When I went for a trial down there just to see if I liked it or not, they were very clever.

They put me in the Ladbrokes shop in Henley for my trial week.

Everybody knows Henley is a very, very, very nice place, so imagine going from working in betting shops in the grotty city centre of Manchester to the lovely, picturesque Henley.

The grade 9 shops are the worst shops in the worst areas, Newton Heath, Miles Platting, etc. My customers were frequently on Crimewatch and would steal anything not nailed down, including the toilet roll.

In Henley they spoke to you respectfully and even said “good morning” and exchanged pleasantries.

So, I went. I transferred to Reading from Manchester and that suppose that was the start of it all.

My parents were quite upset to be honest because nobody- **NOBODY** in my family had ever moved away before- and hardly any since.

They were hurt I think that I wanted to move away, asking what was wrong with Manchester etc. I think they just didn't understand. When I was with my husband who was far from his family in Hong Kong one of the arguments that we used to have sometimes was this: He would say-

“You don't understand how I think- if you have only lived in one place your mind is narrower”.

He was correct- It is narrow.

You can't help it because you haven't had the experience of other places or how foreigners feel.

He was right anyway, and I went to live in Reading.

I know it's not like it is not another country but believe me it felt like another country at the time. Even just going from the North to the South or the UK there are differences in everything.

The lifestyle, the people, the sense of humour, the culture etc

I received an instant promotion so I went from a grade nine shop straight into a grade five shop because they could not ever find people to work in even the good shops in Reading at the time. For this reason, it was difficult to find good managers.

My new Reading supervisor said to me –

"It´s a little bit rough this shop".

Hmm, not compared to the inner-city Manchester shops I had worked in where your customers were on Crimewatch...

I loved it. There were a couple of difficult customers, and difficult staff too to be honest, but I soon got rid of them and settled into it.

The previous manager had been sacked for letting the customers have whatever prices they wanted, so they were not happy with me as I was much stricter on this.

I didn´t want to be sacked.

Eventually they became respectful that I was firm but fair, within reason I would give them a little leeway but not a drastic amount.

Time passed, I loved living in Reading. I made friends; I started a relationship with my supervisor. This too was a disaster, but we are still friends today 30 odd years later so he was in my life for a reason I believe.

By now I was starting to think I just couldn´t do relationships. I always picked the wrong guy somehow, and I got restless so easily and could not settle into a steady relationship. I think this is a result of insecurity maybe, many issues from my childhood that I won´t go into here, but commitment was definitely a big problem for me.

I was always happier alone than in a couple.

CHAPTER 4- A NEW LIFE

As time went on, I started to think about my future. I did not want to be a Ladbrokes manager forever.

The next “career step” in that company was Supervisor. However, they did not earn that much more money and they had an awful lot more responsibility. They were just glorified managers from what I could see.

I investigated coming out of the shops and into a more office-based role. Human resources or something similar, but it transpired that this was nearly as boring as working at the Department of Health and Social Security.

I think in my life I have been cursed with a restless spirit, whenever I have achieved something, I have set my sights on something else. This is not necessarily a positive thing as far as security is concerned. Still, at that time I was still young, and I only had myself to think about, and my little black toy poodle, Zak, so one day I literally just decided to go back into education.

I had left education in my teens because I wanted to earn money and go out to party with my friends. Now I was thinking maybe I would quite like to study more, to go to university. I had got my partying fix and I was slowly recovering from the devastation of losing my best friend Elaine and separating from my husband.

I started to make enquires, and I found an Access course at Reading Technological College that I could take for a year to qualify for university. When I had been at college before I had quite liked Sociology, so I decided to apply to do a degree in this subject. I left Ladbrokes and took a part time job at a small independent bookmaker that fitted in with my Access course.

I was so lucky as education was free then, and I received a mature students grant that combined with my earning was plenty to support myself. That is another terrible thing the Tory Government has done to England, more benefits removed from young people, more opportunities lost.

I did really well in the access course and the following year I started my Sociology degree at Reading University.

I hated it. The Sociology department at Reading was extreme right- wing, almost fascist. My tutor was a woman who dressed like a sex worker and adored Mrs Thatcher, so this was never going to work for me.

Again, I was so lucky.

At Reading University, uniquely, in your first three months you had to choose two other subjects to study as well as your main one. The after the three months you took an exam in each and decided which one to continue with. I guess this is due to the high dropout rate in the first year as students realise the course is not what they expected, or the department is not to their political taste.

The other two subjects I chose were History and Politics and Modern International Relations. I chose Politics as a last resort, I needed one mote subject and I was stuck. I never expected to enjoy it.

I bloody loved it. The Politics Department was modern and forward thinking. It had a good mixture of lecturers of all political persuasion.

I found it all fascinating, the combination of history and politics. British, Russian, American. The history of the Second World War and the Holocaust. The Russian Revolution. The creation of the National health Service and Britain´s first Socialist Government. Britain as the reluctant European.

All these things are pivotal to how society is today. People often say they are not interested in politics, that they do not affect them. I just always think this is the most ridiculous thing to say.

Politics affect our whole lives, from the most important things like employment, health, and education to the price of your pint/glass of wine or the petrol you put in your tank.

And I enjoyed every minute of it.

Everyone should have the opportunity to experience University, not just people lucky enough to be able to afford it. I do not mean only the social aspect but the experience of being part of something and appreciated as such.

I was 30 when I started University, and I had been out in the big wide world working for a huge company like Ladbrokes, who did not really care for your welfare but just your ability to earn money for them.

University is a big bubble where you are listened to, cared for, you have a personal tutor that helps you when you have problems.

The lecturers loved us mature students because we took it seriously, we weren´t just fulfilling our destiny that mummy and daddy were paying for, just to get an average degree to enter a job in the City.

Nobody in my working-class family had ever been to University before, it was far beyond the knowledge of my parents- their ethos was get some basic qualifications so you can get a job- vocations were a luxury they could not afford nor understand... Very irritatingly, they always referred to it as “college”.

My mum-

- How´s college going love?
- When are your holidays from college?
- Have you been to college today?

Me-

-It´s not college, mum, it´s University

My mum-

- I know, you know what I mean.

Next time we spoke, my mum-

- Are you still enjoying college?

I just gave up in the end, it always sounded like I was being snobby. I think she just couldn´t get her head around it, bless her.

My time on the Access course and at University (not college) was probably the most enjoyable time of my life. However, it was during this time another very traumatic event happened.

Not many laughs in this section so just a little warning that if you are feeling particularly sensitive today is probably best not to read on now.

CHAPTER 5- BEING STALKED

According to https://www.stalkingprotectionorder.org/am-i-being-stalked.htmlStalking *is*
A pattern of unwanted behaviour that involves monitoring, harassing, repeatedly contacting or following another person.

Again, where to start is the problem.

This sad story began before the Access course and University and is key to understand how I ever ended up in Spain in the first place.

In Manchester I had a big range of friends and a good social life. All of us who worked for Ladbrokes would meet up on a Thursday to drink, play pool darts and crib, and get to know each other. When I moved to Reading, I had to rebuild my social structure and the first thing I learned was that people there generally were not quite so sociable.

People who worked at Ladbrokes shops only metres from each other did not meet except at staff meetings at head office. They never went to the pub together. One manager I met at a staff meeting was called Terry. He one day did ask me to go for a drink with him. I wanted to go because I missed that social life, and I did think there would be other people there.

There weren´t.

We passed a pleasant evening, but as we parted, he tried to kiss me.

I was startled because for me it was normal to go out with guys from work without there being anything behind it.

Also, I knew that he was married and that was really the last thing I needed, that kind of complication. I think his reaction to my rejection was really a foreboding of the future. Even in those early days maybe I should have read the signs better.

I told him, nicely, that I just was not interested in a relationship. I just wanted to go out for a drink, nothing more.

Terry became quite stroppy and insinuated that I had led him on.

So that was the end of that, we did not speak except where necessary for work for quite a long time afterwards.

Looking back, I should have read the signs and stayed well clear, but events unfolded, and I cannot change the past.

Life can only be understood backwards, right?

Life at Ladbrokes went on, I rarely saw Terry. A few strange things started happening though.

Very occasionally I was off sick- an absolute rarity for me as I am one of those people who NEVER takes time off sick unless I am virtually dying, even when I worked for other people.

I hate to let people down.

I know that many other people do not care about this.

New Year's Day at Ladbrokes (which was of course a working day- lots of big meetings), you could take bets on who would ring in sick and leave everyone else to cope understaffed.

I NEVER did.

Maybe it is me who is the fool, but I just couldn´t do it. I felt guilty even when I was genuinely sick.

In these rare occasions a bunch of flowers would be left at my door or a card wishing me to get better soon. (How did he know I was off sick?)

A birthday card (How did he know it was my birthday?)

A Christmas card (fair enough, everyone know it was Christmas)

All hand delivered when I was out or ill in bed.

Even then there was a lot of stalking behaviour.

He later told me that he would often sit in his car in the petrol station opposite my flat and watch my comings and goings, lights going off and on etc.

When he knew that I was out he would ring my phone (landline) just to hear it ring.

That is all quite spooky isn´t it?

Still, I did not know all this at the time.

Time passed, and I think gradually he just wore me down by being so nice to me.

He was attractive and attentive, I don´t really know how it happened but we did start spending some time together, though only as friends.

I think he caught me at a lonely point in life, he was saying all the right things and making me feel special at a time when I did not really feel very special.

Then something else happened that more or less pushed us together.

During that time, I had taken a lodger in the Ladbrokes flat.

She was a young girl (I won´t give her name, as I do not see her now and have no permission to do so).

She was one of the cashiers that I worked with at my shop. She only lived around the corner, but she wanted some independence from her parents. She was in her early twenties; I was probably 28 or 29.

Moving in with me was perfect, because she was away from home but still near enough to be close to her parents.

I had started seeing Terry on a more regular basis, but it was all innocent, at least in my mind.

Friendship nothing more.

Nothing romantic had happened between us, I think he had realised that the best way to continue seeing me was to not push the relationship before I was ready.

We went for drinks, he came round for dinner with another guy (that liked my flatmate), all very casual and fun.

After one such dinner, the following day he rang me to say that as he was taking the other guy home he had commented to Terry:

"I wouldn´t get too hopeful about a relationship with Vicki if I were you"

When Terry had asked him to expand on that comment he had refused, just saying:

- "Ask Vicki" and repeating his advice.

During the time I was getting closer to Terry my flatmate had started to act a little strangely.

She was saying that she did not like him, she did not see what I saw in him, etc.

Many snide comments that I basically just ignored. Nothing was serious yet, I was enjoying his company, so I did not really care what she said. After this comment by the guy who had come to dinner, and spent quite a lot of time with her, I decided to sit her down and try to find out exactly what the problem was.

We started to talk, and I had concluded by then that maybe she liked him herself. I could not think of any other reason she was so negative about him, he always tried to be nice to her from what I could see.

Eventually I just asked her straight:

“Is it because you like him yourself?” I asked.

“No”- she replied- “It´s because I think that I am in love with you…”

Stunned does not describe how I felt.

This was a girl with whom I had discussed men often.

Boyfriends, exes, who we fancied, who we didn´t.

I had absolutely no reason to believe that she was interested in women.

How long had she thought like this?

She was also the girl that had hung my underwear out on the line many times.

She was the girl that had asked me to read her tarot cards about a subject she would not divulge, but that had always read that it would not lead to anything good.

We had planned holidays together, had even talked about getting a mortgage together.

We had moved from the Ladbrokes flat when I left that employment into a new rental and signed the contract together.

When the hell was she planning to tell me?

I was even more stunned when it transpired that she had told virtually everyone except me about this.

Her friends, even the guy who had come to dinner, hence his cryptic comment to Terry advising him to not get his hopes up for any relationship with me.

Of all the reasons that had occurred to me that she might be disapproving of my relationship with Terry this had not been one of them.

When I spoke to Terry later that day to tell him how it went, he said:

"Don´t tell me, she is in love with me"

I said:

- "No, actually she is in love with me"

That was a bit of a blow for his ego, I think.

I had a good friend at the time that was in a gay relationship. I asked her and her girlfriend to take my flatmate around some of the gay clubs in the area so that she could explore if she was gay or not.

I think in hindsight she had a sort of schoolgirl crush on me rather than a sexual thing. She did not like the gay scene and she later married an older guy from work and had children.

I should mention that Terry was also a lot older than me, 16 years to be precise, maybe she was emulating me, I really do not know.

All I know is that I felt very butch for a long time afterwards, as I did not understand why she thought I might be gay.

I like women of course, and I can appreciate their beauty and find them attractive. But sexually they do absolutely nothing for me whatsoever. Sometimes I wonder if my love life might have been easier if they did- but they don´t.

If you are reading this, my ex-flatmate, I hope that your life has been happy and fulfilled.

We were good friends and we did have many good times together, until and even after that bombshell.

However, I do sort of blame her for what happened next. I could not afford the rent on the new flat on my own when she moved out due to the situation.

So-she moved out and Terry moved in, and that´s when our relationship started.

In the year or so we had been friends, Terry had always told me what I suppose is the classic married man´s story. That he and his wife had been like brother and sister for years, she had told him to leave many times, and it was just a question of finding somewhere appropriate to live.

He said that she was actively encouraging him to leave.

I was a lot younger then, and I just believed him. All you wives out there who like to blame the other woman if your husband has had an affair, I know it must hurt and is probably easier to blame a stranger, but I never understand it.

I would always put the blame on the man that was supposed to be married to me for better or worse. They lie to their "girlfriend", who is likely younger and more naïve, and she takes pity on him for his unfortunate situation. In my opinion the sympathy often lies erroneously with the pathetic husband who just could.t help himself, lured away by some siren.

In my opinion a man is not much of a man if he allows this to happen.

And in my experience the man goes all out to start and sustain the affair, until he gets caught then suddenly, he is the victim.

Anyway, regardless of what anyone believes our romantic relationship did not start until Terry left his wife.

Predictably, the things he had told me turned out not actually to be true. His wife was livid when he left, not relieved at all, and blamed me completely for wrecking her marriage.

I have to say that in the beginning our relationship was good overall.

It was nice to go out with an older man who adored me and would do anything for me. We seemed so compatible, we liked doing all the same things.

Now I wonder if he really liked doing them or just would do anything to please me.

I am an early morning person and was out at the crack of dawn to walk with the dog, as I still do now.

I was (believe it or not ⍰), a keep-fit fanatic at the time who played squash, jogged, went to circuit training, step, and the gym.

We went rambling every weekend, long walks whatever the weather.

Terry, well into his forties, joined in with everything. I later realised that it was because he would not let me do anything alone, nor even with my female friends.

He had to watch me every minute he was so insecure.

However, things were good for a while.

I was doing the Access course at Reading college and working weekends at the Independent Bookmakers.

Terry left Ladbrokes and came to work there as well. Another sign really.

Before we got together, he had lots of guy friends he would go playing cards with or to the races etc.

He stopped doing all that.

He never stopped me going anywhere, but he would always make me feel guilty about it, leaving him alone. Even just going to the gym with my friend Martine.

When she came to pick me up, he would say:

"Are you taking her away from me again? - and she would feel uncomfortable.

Problems really started when I went to university.

He enjoyed chatting to me about the subjects on that course as he was interested in the subjects too.

However, when I went to university it was all a bit over his head.

Really if you weren´t doing the course it would be for anyone.

I wouldn´t like to sit and talk about University Level Mathematics or any other subject unless I was taking it myself.

However, as he did not like me doing things on my own, he would insist on coming along to any social gatherings or parties.

Then he would complain that I hadn´t included him enough in the conversation. The conversation obviously was all about the course as that was what we had in common.

I joined the Labour Party and started attending meetings. So did he. It was the beginning of the Blair years I suppose or just before.

I remember it was Terry that told me that John Smith had had a heart attack and died one day when I rang him at work. We were heartbroken, we all thought he would be the next Prime Minister.

Another thing that did not help our relationship was when I left the Independent Bookmakers that he had followed me to and started working for the Tote on Course bookmakers on racecourses at weekends and holidays.

I loved that job. It was so different from the betting shops as people were on a day out and much happier. Ascot, Windsor, Bath, Chepstow, Goodwood, Cheltenham etc. We travelled all over and sometimes we stayed overnight or even for a week if it was a big meeting.

It wasn´t fabulous in the way of well-paid particularly, it was just fun and a great atmosphere.

I had to work to supplement my grants and to help pay our bills.

He was working of course, but then we bought a house together, so we had a mortgage to pay.

Also, we paid maintenance for his three teenage daughters.

Terry was not abusive, but he was controlling.

He was constantly asking me to marry him, I am just grateful that I didn´t.

I believe that once he thought he was finally secure with me that he would have ramped up his control. Anyone who has ever had that sort of relationship will know that it does not go bad overnight, it happens gradually.

So gradually that you don´t even realise it is happening until you are too entwined in it.

"Jokey" comments, turning up unexpectedly at race meetings that I was working at to "surprise" me, reading my diary, going through the bins to see what I had thrown away.

Not physical abuse, but it was a possessiveness that over time made me feel suffocated and that I could not breathe and be myself. I felt guilty every time I left him or tried to do anything on my own.

It got worse and worse, and my mental health started to suffer. I was having panic attacks on a regular basis.

During one, when I was really down, Terry suggested that we commit suicide together.

Another day, during an argument, he locked himself in the garage in our back yard and started stringing up a noose.

He told me that he had been suicidal since his teenage years but had never followed it through.

His mother later told me that his father was an abusive alcoholic and that these feelings had started then.

All this was chipping away at our relationship and my relationships with other people. Terry wanted to do things but just wanted to be me and him. It was almost comical when it was coming up to bonfire night and I would want to go to a big, organised fireworks display, and he would just want to be in the back garden with a couple of Catherine wheels - just me and him and sparklers.

I was 32 years old, and I still had a lot of dreams.

One was having children.

Until I hit thirty I hadn´t really thought about it much, but after thirty my hormones must have kicked in or something, because I really wanted them. A little while after Terry and I had moved in together I had been late with my period and got quite excited that I might have been pregnant. When I shared this with him, he said:

- "What do you mean? You can't be pregnant, I´m sterile".

He had not shared this fact with me before we got together.

Years before, Terry had had Hodgkin's Lymphoma and had been given only months to live.

He was saved by a course of chemotherapy during which he lost all his hair, and his sperm count too. At the time he was offered the opportunity to freeze some sperm, but as he was already married with three young daughters, he did not accept the offer.

I knew that he had had chemo, but I did not know it could make you sterile.

He insinuated that I should have known and was quite dismissive about it.

He went for tests, and it was confirmed, he was sterile.

I was devastated. This was another crack in the wall of our relationship. I felt hurt he had not been honest with me, he know I wanted children and although he had not lied, he had withheld the truth.

We were placed on a list for artificial insemination for when I finished my degree. The specialist assured me they matched the fathers' physical characteristics with the donor and said that they were normally medical students so presumably they would have a reasonable level of intelligence.

There were a lot of things I did like about our relationship. I felt secure being with someone who seemingly loved me so much, but my anxiety and panic attacks were ramping up. However, if he could just have been less possessive maybe it would have turned out ok.

I still had this image that I would one day would like to go and live abroad and my dream at this time when I was so interested politics was to work for the European Union in Brussels.

It seems ironic now after the disaster that is Brexit.

Terry complained that every job I ever said I wanted was abroad and would take me away from him.

He did not understand that I had wanted to live abroad since I was a little girl and there was no reason why he could not come with me.

So, these were the several reasons that our relationship was starting to unravel.

We were starting to grow apart, and we both know it.

September 1995 my friend Martine came to see me with exciting news. I had met Martine whilst working at Ladbrokes and we had become good friends. She had since left Ladbrokes and working in the NHS. She had married and started a family when very young and had long wanted to separate from her husband. Her children were now adults and she had finally left him.

One night she had been out for dinner with her brother-in-law, and he had told her that he had three villas in Spain that he had bought during the Thatcher boom. During the Thatcher recession he had let them go a bit, he was a builder and had suffered greatly. The water and electricity were off, the community fees had not been paid, but there was no mortgage owing.

They needed sorting out to be rented now that things were improving, and he offered her the opportunity to live free of charge in one of the smaller ones if she did this for him, whilst renting the others out.

Martine was hoping for an escape I suppose and she jumped at the chance. She was going over for a week first to get the water and electricity sorted and I immediately offered to go with her. My last year at University did not start until the end of September- We booked our flights and that was it.

Terry wasn´t particularly happy but we were not at a point yet where we were completely tied to each other, i.e., married, so there was not much he could do. I remember he tried to make me jealous inventing all these things he was planning to do while I was away.

I really didn´t care I just couldn´t wait to get away and get some sun.

So off we went. We had a fantastic time. I had never been to mainland Spain and apart from the fact the weather was perfect (September generally is), I felt I had been released from prison.

I did not behave myself that week I´m afraid to say. I acted like a single woman. We both behaved like teenagers and had a ball.

That's the first and last time in my life that I have ever been unfaithful to anyone. The only excuse I have is the suffocation I had felt and the freedom I experienced on arriving in Spain.

On the plane going back Martine asked me:

- “What are you going say to Terry when you get back”.

I replied:

“Nothing, it will all be fine”.

You know when you say you are fine but in fact you are not fine at all.

Terry came to meet us at the airport.

I took one look at him, and I knew I had to leave him.

I am a person who wears my heart on my sleeve, I just could not pretend any more. This has been the bane of my life really, not being able to pretend or have a poker face. There was just no way I could carry on our relationship, the guilt I felt was unbearable.

It was a Friday, and I was working the next day at Ascot racecourse. I told him I needed some breathing space, and I would go straight from work to stay with my niece Michelle in London. After work I set off.

Maybe if he had given me this breathing space, things would have been different. But he couldn´t. That´s really when the whole saga set into motion towards what now seems like an inevitable conclusion.

On the M4 there was a massive traffic jam.

Whilst I was stuck in it with no end in sight my mobile rang. It was Terry. He said that he had taken an overdose and if I didn´t come straight back he would die. I could not even move the traffic was so bad.

Finally, I rang my sister who rang the Samaritans, and they went around to the house. I knew the Reading Samaritans personally as I had been a volunteer there myself for 2 years.

An ambulance was called but Terry refused to go to hospital and the paramedics decided there was not a serious threat to his life and went. My friend the Samaritan sat with him for a while, then eventually Terry himself said he was ok.

It sounds awful, but I then knew for sure I had made the right decision. I could not be blackmailed into going back to him. That and his subsequent actions drove me further away from him, not back towards him.

He did not have the telephone number of my niece thankfully.

I would ring him and withhold my number. However, he had stolen my address book before I left and he was constantly ringing my parents, my family, and friends to try and get the number and my address. I continued living at my nieces for quite a while, but the travelling from Reading to Edmonton just got more and more wearing.

The distance was not that far, it was the traffic.

Eventually a fellow student, a single parent called Alison offered me her spare room to help me out and help her with the costs. It was a win-win situation.

I obviously did not tell Terry that I had moved back to Reading, though he tried his best to find out where I was.

He would ring my friends in a panic, saying that something terrible had happened and he had to speak to me urgently. Or my parents or other family members. They had all been briefed that under no circumstances should they give him my number. That they should contact me, and I would ring from a withheld number.

Life carried on.

Gradually he did seem to be accepting that we would not get back together.

At least seemed to be.

He had even answered some "Lonely hearts" adverts and had some dates. I did feel a fleeting jealousy, which I suppose is what he wanted, but at heart I was relieved that he was moving on.

My friend and I were planning a Christmas trip to Spain, a month over Christmas and New Year, before she planned to move out there for good the following Spring. Terry said he was worried about me, and he offered to take my car for some new tyres, as we were to be driving there.

I let him. This new friendship was great, and it was good to see him so upbeat, quite happy with the new woman he was seeing.

Why shouldn´t we be friends helping each other out?

Just before we went away in the December of 1995 there was a meeting at Cheltenham that I attended. We stayed over for the week, The night before we returned home, we all went out and got merrily drunk and I spent the night in a nice hotel with a guy that I had worked with for 2 years.

Funnily enough I had never really liked him, and I thought he didn´t like me.

He was also a terrible womaniser and I just didn´t find that appealing. However, that night he made an orchestrated effort to impress me, and it worked. I was full of my newfound freedom and the awareness that I was free to do whatever I liked.

A week later Martine and I set off to Spain in my car.

We took turns driving.

Martine is one of those lucky people who can sleep in a car whereas I am not.

So for me it was a long journey.

We did it all in one hit (24 hours), we just could not wait to get here.

In about the second week we were there Martine and I had an argument.

We had never had one before and we have never had one since. My period was due, and I blamed my irritability on this fact, but Martine said immediately-

"-I think that you are pregnant".

This was a total shock to me to even consider it, I had lived for so long with a guy who was sterile and had not even had to think about birth control. I was in denial.

At the same time, I was in contact regularly with one of my nieces Joanne who was also "late". I was telling her to take a pregnancy test and she now started telling me to do the same. The niece I had lived with briefly, Michelle, was getting married in August 1996. I was to be matron of honour and Joanne her sister was to be a bridesmaid. Neither of us made it.

I bought my pregnancy test eventually in the first week of the new year from a supermarket in Torrevieja that was called Continente and is now Carrefour.

When it turned out positive, I threw it to the other side of the room, I just could not believe it. Bear in mind that this is the girl who thought she was never going to get pregnant because she had a partner who was sterile.

Also, as I had not previously conceived with any partner I had, and had never in fact used birth control, I had started to think well maybe I can't have children.

It seems silly now but seriously, I had almost forgotten about the possibility of getting pregnant. Although it was by no means a perfect situation I was absolutely thrilled. I just could not wait to get back home and see my doctor to make sure that everything was ok. I immediately stopped smoking and drinking.

So, we set off back home. Just over the French border the car broke down.

You will read a blog post later in this book which talks of other bad experiences I have had in France; it is like a black hole for me where everything goes wrong.

We had literally just crossed the border and stopped to get some petrol as it was just getting dark, and then the car just died. Luckily in the garage not on the road.

Also luckily, I had roadside assistance with Green Flag. A "grua" came to get us, a French guy obviously and a bit surly.

He drove us out into the middle of nowhere and we were actually quite scared for a while, as it was pitch black and we had no idea where we were going.

We arrived at a garage, and we were given two choices. Stay in a hotel until the car was ready, which would be a few days as it was a weekend. Or stay just one night and we would get a hire car the next day to take us back home, then Green Flag would fly someone over to get my car and bring it home. I must say, I was very impressed with their service and if they are still in existence, I would definitely recommend them.

We stayed one night, then took the car hire option.

We had so much stuff and it was left to Martine to do most of the lifting as I of courses was pregnant and couldn´t. She had to do it all again at Calais and then again at Dover as we were not allowed to take the French hire car over the channel and had to get on the ferry as foot passengers. It is a bit of a standing joke now between is how she had to lift everything. I had never been pregnant before and I did act a bit like a delicate flower. I was so scared of losing this baby I was so happy to at last be carrying.

It sounds so dramatic, but any of you ladies reading this who have longed for a baby and thought you could not have one will understand. It becomes a kind of obsession, and when it finally happens you just cannot believe it.

I always felt that something would go wrong, and I would never see this babies face.

Once home, I made my appointment at the doctors.

There was a heart stopping moment when at first, she could not find the heartbeat, but then suddenly there it was.

There is nothing quite like hearing that for the first time.

I did not care that I was not in a relationship with the father, I did not care that I would be a single mother, I did not care about any of it. I was just delighted to be pregnant.

The father was married, and we literally had only been together one time. I did briefly think about making up a father, but I knew I would never be able to sustain a lie. The truth always comes out in the end. I was dreading telling him and I was dreading telling Terry but none of that diminished my delight in being pregnant. Although I will talk about the father in this book, I will never mention his real name.

A week went by and the guy from Green Flag jumped on an aeroplane and went to collect my newly repaired car. He delivered it directly to my door, to the house I was sharing with my fellow student. Late that evening I was chatting with one of my sisters on the telephone. As I was doing so, something came through the letterbox.

I just assumed that it was a leaflet of some kind, though I remember thinking that it was quite late to be delivering leaflets. When I finished the call, I went over to see what it was.

It was not a leaflet. It was a letter. From Terry.

In the letter he told me in no uncertain terms that he was taking the car as it was half his and he wanted it. When he had (as I thought kindly) taken the car to get the tyres changed for my trip to Spain he had also had a copy of the keys made. He would return the car when I came back to live with him.

It was apparent that all those weeks I thought that he was moving on in fact he hadn´t. And how had he found out where I lived?

When we had split up the arrangement had been that I would keep the car as I needed it to get to University from London, and he would keep the house. I don´t know what shocked me most, the fact that he had sneakily had keys cut whilst pretending to do me a favour or that he had somehow managed to track me down.

The following day I went to his place of work and kicked up enough fuss, threatening to phone the police, to make him tell me where it was. The car was in my name at least, He had parked it in a hidden cul -de- sac where I would never have found it and had even put a crook lock on it.

I got my car back. However, I had now more idea of the lengths he would go to find out where I was living and make my life difficult. I had changed my address with the Labour Party, and he had gone to the Secretary of my branch, a mutual friend, with some cock and bull story and the idiot had told him the new address.

Chris apologised profusely but I was fuming that he had done that. He could have put me in real danger. He told me that Terry was like a bloodhound in his quest to find out where I was, it was all he talked about. He constantly badgered him and eventually he had given in.

Great- this could have been very dangerous for me.

I had to move again, back to my nieces in London. I was starting to get a very bad feeling about how all this was going to end up. It was now the end of January 1996, four months from when we had split up.

Despite having met someone else Terry did not seem to be moving on, and due to the sneaky way he had acted over the car and finding out where I was, I was becoming increasingly paranoid.

He was still constantly ringing my friends and family. I was dreading having to tell him I was pregnant. It was ridiculous though; we had been apart 4 months and really it was nothing to do with him.

The only time he would know where I was for sure was when I was working at a racecourse. He knew the ones I always attended. I would come to the car park and even check the boot of my car to make sure he was not in there before I drove off, that's how paranoid I was.

Terry had left his first wife for his second wife and his second wife for me. But I was not allowed to leave him.

He told all my friends and family that I was mentally unbalanced but eventually I would come to my senses. I went to the police to stop him harassing me through my friends and family and was told they could not do anything unless he harmed me physically.

I believe nowadays there are more laws protecting victims of stalkers, many women die at the hands of ex partners every year.

According to Refuge, on average two women a week are killed by current or ex partners in England and Wales alone.

Still people do not take it seriously. I was totally staggered not that long ago, when a 30-year-old girl I had working with me as a receptionist said she did not believe women who said they were being stalked, she thought they were being dramatic and overreacting.

Unbelievable. I hope for her sake she never experiences any kind of stalking behaviour.

It is a horrible feeling to be stalked, impossible to explain. Even my own friends and family did not understand my uneasiness and feeling of not being safe, probably amplified by the fact I was pregnant. They would say;

"-Terry would never hurt you; he loves you"

I was 100 percent certain that he would hurt me if he got the chance and he thought there was no hope of us getting back together.

I remembered vividly when he suggested that we commit suicide together. I was not safe, and my baby was not safe either.

Finally, I told him that I was pregnant. I told him that the father was someone that I had met on holiday, and I had no contact with him. I could not tell him the truth about my work friend because he knew him.

Funnily enough, he was delighted. He thought that this was the answer to all our problems. I had wanted a baby and now I was having one- he would bring it up as if it was his own and we would all live happily ever after.

I will be honest and say there were times that I considered it. It was daunting knowing that I would be a single parent. I still had not told the father and I was dreading his reaction. I was considering not even telling him at all. One evening I went to dinner with Terry at one of our favourite restaurants. I had to see if I had any feeling left and if there was any possibility that we could continue our relationship. There wasn´t, I just knew that I couldn´t do it.

He said a disgusting thing to me that I do not even feel comfortable repeating, and I had my answer right then and there.

When I dropped him off at the house, he asked me to come in as he bought me some of my favourite cheesecake.

I declined. I would not want to be alone with him in the house, I just couldn´t wait to get away.

We were now in February.

I was still living at my niece Michelle´s house in Edmonton and travelling to university.

It was wearing.

Monday 13th February 1996, I felt quite sick when I got up and I just could not face the trip.

I called the University and said I would not be in that day.

Someone somewhere was looking over me. That morning, a friend from university called me. She told me that Terry was wandering around the University in a terrible state. Crying, asking anyone if they knew where I was.

She had tried to calm him down and told him she would ring me and ask me to call him. He should go home and calm down or go to work.

Terry by then was running his own bookmaker's shop that his mum had given him money for. That evening I called him and withheld the number. He was at home, he was calmer, but he said that if I did not come back there and then he would kill himself.

Of course, I could not go there. There was no way that I would go there. I tried my best to talk to him, but he had only one thing to say:

-"Come here now or I will kill myself."

I said to him that I would ring his sister and ask her to call him, but that I was not coming. His last words to me were "I hope I see you on the other side".

I rang his sister and told her the situation. What should I do?

She said she would call him then call me back to see how it went. I said tell him that I will ring him in the morning.

She rang back about an hour later and said that he seemed better.

He said that he would not do anything, and she told him that both of us would ring him the next day. Valentines' day, February 14th, 1996.

We both felt there was not much else that we could do.

She did not live nearby either, she lived about 2 hours away. It was now late, maybe midnight. We agreed to go to bed and speak again in the morning.

I could not sleep, only doze. I was tortured by fears that maybe he had found out where I was and was on his way over to kill me.

A murder suicide.

You might feel that sound dramatic or ridiculous, but if you had been in my position, you may have felt differently. I know he was unhinged I just did not know what to do about it.

If you have read my blogs, you will know that I believe in spirituality, things happen that we cannot account for.

At around four am that morning I was awoken with a start. I had a vision, or a dream, I do not know which. I saw a hooded figure vey sadly waiting for Terry. My stomach flipped over, and I knew at that moment he was no longer on this earth.

I got up and started to call him. No answer. No answer no answer.

My niece got up; her boyfriend went off to work. I just kept calling, still no answer.

At 9 he was supposed to be at work, so I alternated my calls between the 2 places. Still no answer. I rang his sister; she got no answer either.

I knew something had happened. My niece kept insisting that he was probably just making me worry so that I would go round there. I knew in my heart that was not the case.

I rang the Reading police and explained to situation to them. They went to his shop to find it closed. Then they went to the house. They rang me to say the back door was open and they had gone in and found nothing. They told me not to worry, he had likely gone for a walk somewhere to clear his head.

So, I just kept ringing. No answer, no answer.

Suddenly, the line was engaged. A little bit of hope flared in my heart.

Engaged, engaged, engaged.

See, my niece said, he is probably on the phone to his sister.

Finally, it rang through, and the phone was answered.

It was not Terry; it was the police. A woman.

She asked who I was, and I told her. As we were not married, she was very reluctant to give details at first, as technically I was not family. However, I explained to her that that was our shared house and finally she asked me for the dog´s name.

My little poodle Zak had stayed with Terry because I could not take him to my niece's house. The policewoman told me that they could not get into the room "where Terry was" because Zak was guarding him.

I asked if he had hung himself in the garage, and she confirmed that this was indeed what he had done. It was the dog howling next to his body that had alerted them on leaving the house that there was another part of the house that they had not checked.

I remember running out into the street, the air was freezing but I felt dizzy and sick, I took great gulps of it. My heart was thumping, and my stomach was churning. I was terrified that I might have a miscarriage. The finality of what had happened was overwhelming. However, the profound sadness I felt was accompanied also by a sense of relief. This is an awful thing to admit, and judge me as you will, but there was a lot of relief that it was over, my baby and I were safe, he was not coming to get us.

To this day I still have recurring nightmares that he is knocking on my window or coming up my path, angry and tearful as he was on that last night, and I wake in a cold sweat.

As the dream fades and I realise that it not real, I get that same sense of relief that I had that morning.

Terry´s brother turned up on the scene, he had spoken to his sister and driven down from Portsmouth to see if he was ok. To him fell the unenviable task of identifying Terry´s body.

Suicide is a terrible thing. It affects everyone in the victim's life. It is of course unbearably sad that someone felt so desperate to take their own life, but it is a choice too. It can be an act of anger, revenge. Terry had three teenage girls and the effect on them must have been devastating. I had a very good relationship with his family and his mother told me that he had been insecure and had suicidal tendencies all his life. Terry himself told me he had considered it many times especially when he had cancer, but he did not want his daughters to find him dead.

His mother also told me that he had tried hard to step back and leave me alone but that he just could not do it. He was obsessed. She dd not blame me, but of course I blamed myself.

Suicide sort of sucks you in, it gives you suicidal feelings too. Luckily for me, I had my baby to think of and I put all my energies into finishing my degree and preparing for the arrival of my baby,

I moved back into our house, which was difficult.

However, he had not killed himself in the house itself, so it was bearable. I never went into the garage.

Many things I found there showed me the state of mind he was in and how dangerous that he was. Journals, phone logs, etc. I will not go into details, but he was very unbalanced, the coroner also informed me of some things that they had taken away that clearly showed his disturbed state of mind.

I learnt that he also had many financial problems too.

I often wonder about the woman he was seeing, if she knew what happened or if she just wondered why he stopped contacting her.

The first few nights I slept back there my friend Martine stayed with me, then I was coping, and she moved back home.

The first night I slept back in our bed I felt a tight embrace of someone putting their arms around me and hugging tightly. I knew that was Terry. I know many of you will not believe these things, but I do. It only happened once but I was awake, not asleep, and I felt it physically.

I have had a few other experiences over the years, but I won´t go into them all now.

There was an inquest, I had to give evidence. It was awful. The verdict was suicide, and it was even a headline in the local paper,

"Broken-hearted Bookie Takes His Own Life"

Terry, I hope you are at peace.

I took some time off work, but I knew that sooner or later I would also have to face the father of my unborn child and tell him that I was pregnant...

CONFESSIONS OF A SPANISH TEACHER

Vicki Marie Riley

CHAPTER 6- THE FATHER

I will never forget how the father found out.

I had planned to tell him at an opportune time, but as I had been off work this just had not happened yet. People at the Head Office knew what had happened to Terry and one of them, a friend Janice, knew that I was pregnant as I had had to provide a sick note for my time off.

My first day back was an evening meeting at Windsor, one of my favourite racecourses,

Everyone seemed very surprised when the father of my baby (from now I will call him Patrick) turned up although he in fact was not working that day. I like to think he turned up because he had heard about Terry and was worried about my welfare. He came over and chatted, asked how I was, and stayed to help out for the whole meeting.

At one point before racing started Janice came up to us as we were chatting and asked:

“Have you had any morning sickness?”.

Patrick´s jaw dropped. And he looked at me questioningly.

“Ah yes”- I said- “and on top of everything else, I´m pregnant”.

It wasn´t the way I would have chosen to tell him.

The evening continued, and to give Patrick his due he stayed until the end even though technically he wasn´t even supposed to be working. He was white- faced and looked completely shell-shocked. You could just see the cogs turning and I expect he was doing quite a lot of calculating with dates.

Poor guy. I did feel for him, but I knew he did put it around a bit, so I suppose it was inevitable to happen eventually. Maybe it had already happened with someone else. He had not taken any precautions to stop it happening, let´s put it that way.

The next time I worked was at Ascot and I was put in a tiny shop working alone upstairs in the Member´s enclosure. I think this was deliberate as Patrick appeared almost immediately and asked me straight out if the baby was his.

I replied that he should not ask that question unless he was really sure that he would like to know the answer. He said he would like to know before anyone else found out.

My biggest fear was that he would ask me to have an abortion, so I pre-empted him by saying-

“Don´t ask me to have an abortion”.

To his credit, he seemed mortified by the suggestion. Patrick was a Catholic.

“Oh no,” he said-

“This is a life, I would never ask that, I just need to know what you want from me?”

I reassured him that I was not expecting him to leave his wife, just maybe some moral and financial support would be useful. He agreed, and I have always thought he was secretly quite thrilled. He was 10 years older than me, well into his forties, and I do think he saw it as some proof that there was “life in the old dog yet”.

Bless him. For me, I will always be eternally grateful for the son he gave me, even if it was an unexpected event.

I loved being pregnant. Everyone treats you so nicely. They open doors for you, ask about your welfare and carry things for you. This strangely enough does not continue after you actually have the baby. Struggling with a pushchair, doors slam in your face and people seem surprised that you should even be out of the house letting your baby cry and irritate them. In the UK at least. It is different in Spain I believe.

It was only knowing that I would have to support my baby alone that gave me the strength to finish my degree after the trauma of Terry´s suicide. I took my finals in the sick bay; I was heavily pregnant. I achieved a 2:1 degree, not unfortunately the first-class honours degree I had been tipped for, but I was pleased that I had actually managed to complete it.

At my graduation ceremony I was 8 months pregnant, my baby was due at the end of August. He did not arrive until the 13th of September. I could hardly walk I was like a zeppelin I was so big.

My relationship with Patrick was difficult. I was still working with him and all kinds of rumours were flying around work. He did not seem to have learnt from his mistake.

One absolutely awful day I was subjected to a couple of hours of listening to one of the cashiers relating her escapades with him the night before. All the gory details, positions etc. In the meantime, I was carrying his child. It was a messed-up situation.

I was 2 weeks late and my midwife was starting to worry, and she said that I should be induced. There were 2 slots available, Friday the 13th of September or Monday the 16th. I just did not feel that I could wait the whole weekend, so I went for Friday 13th to get it over with. Lucky for some.

On the morning that I was booked in to be induced, my waters broke. Again, I was fortunate as I had a bed booked at the hospital for inducement. Earlier that year there had been a scare about the safety of taking the pill, and it was a bumper autumn for babies. Women were in labour in the corridors, no beds available, but I had a labour room all to myself.

My son was born without significant incident at 5.55 pm.

I brought him home, deliriously happy.

I just want to mention here another experience that added to my spiritual convictions.

Two weeks after my son was born, my mother fell very ill in Manchester. She had stomach problems and was taken into hospital for investigations. Whilst doing these investigations, her bowel ruptured, and she was rushed into emergency surgery to save her life. My Dad said they were running up the corridor with the gurney, it was so touch and go. A ruptured bowel poisons your system.

She was given a colostomy and sent immediately to Intensive Care, the Doctor said that she had a fifty percent chance of survival. I rushed down (or is it up?) from Reading with my two-week-old son who she had never seen.

It seems amazing now, but I was allowed to take him into the Intensive Care ward where my Mum was lying in an induced coma.

I took her hand and told her: -

- "Mum, you are going to recover because Jack is here, and you are going to see him"

Her eyes flickered.

My mum did recover from that illness, though she would wear a colostomy bag for the rest of her life- which she hated.

When she was conscious, I took Jack in to see her, and she told me of the near-death experience she had had.

She was in a tunnel, with a bright light at the end of it, travelling toward it. In the tunnel there were many other people, and animals too. This will be comforting to any of you out there who love pets, as I do.

She said that suddenly she heard me calling her and she saw Jack and I at the other end of the tunnel. She tried to reach out for us but every time she got near, we would move further and further away. She followed us back along the tunnel away from the light, we moved further away again. This continued until she was back at the other end of the tunnel, but she never quite reached us.

Then she woke up.

Well, we all have our different beliefs so make of it what you will. My Mum was not an imaginative person who made things up. She told me this story as soon as she was able to speak to us, and I take great comfort from it.

This event, combined with many other experiences I have had, reassures me that there are indeed many things we do not understand fully.

Mum, when you finally arrived at the other end of the tunnel, I hope my Dad was there waiting for you or even holding your hand as you travelled down it.

Now my brother Tony has also taken that journey.

I miss you all so much.

CHAPTER 7- SPAIN BECKONS

So here I was, a single mother with a degree in politics, mortgage arrears and a dream to live in Spain. My friend Martine had gone to live in Spain and then come back.

Patrick came to see the baby a couple of times, but not exactly on a regular basis. Just before he died Terry had taken out an extension on a joint loan we had without my permission. The bank informed me that as it had originally been in both our names, he could do that without my signature and that I was now liable for the whole loan. I was on Income support to supplement my part time earning from the Tote, but I was told that as I had a mortgage rather than paid rent, this would not be paid.

My mortgage was 350 pounds a month, they would not pay it- but if I moved into a private rental at 650 pounds a month, they would pay that.

Bloody ridiculous.

I found a buyer for my house, and we planned a trip to Spain for a month.my son was nine months old.

I had a little bit of equity. In this I had not been so lucky as if I had waited a year longer, I would have had a lot more. The economy was improving under the new Labour Government and property values started to increase.

But hey ho, swings and roundabouts. I had enough money to live for a year and I was already thinking that if I found somewhere to live that I would stay in Spain, at least for a while.

I found somewhere.

The month passed and my friend Martine returned to the UK without me. I remember how bereft I felt when she first returned. Sometimes I would see someone like her and get a huge rush of happiness that she had come back, only to feel a crushing loneliness when I realised it was not her. I felt so lonely.

Many times, I thought about returning to the UK. But there were so many questions. Where would I live? Where would I work? Would I see Patrick, would he have any role in my son´s life?

I had a couple of insignificant relationships, nothing worth mentioning.

Social life was all about drinking and bars. No one ever invited you round for a cup of tea, and if they did when you got there you were normally offered wine. If you already have a drink problem Spain is not the place to come and live.

I started playing darts for a local bar. I took my baby everywhere with me which in hindsight probably was not really a good thing to do. I started to learn Spanish, quite half- heartedly at first if I am completely honest. My first year in Spain was really like a big, long holiday I suppose.

Every time I thought about returning to the UK things would happen to keep me there. People would come out to visit, I would find a cheaper place to live and move, lots of different things really.

One “suitor” I had was called Ray.

God bless him he is no longer with us.

He was a fair bit older than me and he took Jack and I under his wing a bit.

Ray had previously been living with a lady Val but they were now apart and had been for some time. I was not interested in him romantically whatsoever, and not really in anyone.

My experience with Terry had put me off relationships and I think still does. I never wanted to feel so responsible for someone else's happiness again.

However, he was good company and he also played darts at the bar where I did. One night after playing, he walked us home and came in for a coffee. Nothing more, he had a coffee and went. The next morning, I came down to my car to find my tyre slashed.

Another resident from my block of flats told me that he had seen Val wandering around in her nightie and listening outside my door. I could never prove it was her, but I did challenge her about it and she practically admitted it. What is with these crazy people?

Ray went on to marry a lovely German lady and returned to the UK. He then put my name forward as a tenant for the nice little villa he had been renting and Jack and I moved in there, where we settled for approximately four years. In that first year we had lived in 4 different accommodations.

I do not know if I made the right decision in coming here, I will never know how my life would have turned out if I had not. I would not have learned Spanish, I would not have written my books on learning Spanish, and I would not be writing this book either.

I have had many lovely experiences in Spain, but it has been tough, especially financially. It is hard to get a good job in this part of Spain and hard to earn enough money to live. Little or no help from the Government so is a constant struggle to make ends meet.

Sometimes things are good, business is doing well. Then the recession or "la crisis" decimated the Spanish economy, especially this area with relies so heavily on tourism. We were just recovering from this when Covid struck, and the double whammy of Covid and Brexit.

Life is difficult, not just for me but for many, many people.

Who knows what is going to happen next?

Here I was, I had finally realised my dream. Did it start with the Vicki that was telling my Dad, “I´m going to live in Spain one day”?

Separating from my husband?

My friend coming here to Spain?

Terry´s suicide?

Having my baby?

It is very difficult to find a clear beginning to any story isn´t it?

I do not know exactly where it all started, but I was here, for better or worse.

CHAPTER 8- LIVING THE DREAM?

I actually do not like the expression “living the dream”. Many people think that living in Spain is some kind of perfect life.

It is not. You have all the same problems as you would anywhere else, is just a warmer and prettier place to have them in. Your problems do not disappear magically, whether financial, health, personal etc. Once I got talking to some holiday makers on the beach and one of the ladies even said:

- “You don´t get illness here, do you?”

Bloody ridiculous.

Unless you are financially secure, life is hard.

No handouts, you have to work hard for everything you have.

And really hard.

You do not have your normal support network of family and friends; you have to make new ones.

You work more hours for less money, it is not all cocktails on the beach.

People who live here can´t usually afford cocktails on the beach, only tourists can. And you have the Language Barrier, which I had too at first.

However, that all said, it is generally cheaper to live here so I suppose everything is relative.

Certainly, eating out etc is very reasonable, so we

do tend to do it more than you would in the UK.

That first year I was here and not yet working was 1997.

There were a couple of significant events.

That year we lost Princess Diana. I am not a Royalist, I am a Republican, but like many others despite this I loved Diana. The morning she died I walked up to a local bar for a coffee, unaware, and saw the news coming through there on the television.

An awful time for anyone British, wherever you were. We watched the funeral at a friend's house, as we had no television.

This friend Chris was also to die a tragic death when a couple of months late he and his brother-in-law were gassed by a faulty gas boiler.

They had been in the bar where his wife was working and gone home just minutes before her. When she arrived home a very short time later, they were both dead, and she barely escaped with her life, coming out of the house on her hands and knees.

Carbon Monoxide poisoning.

If you have an inside gas boiler, I would recommend either moving it outside or changing it to electric. I would not have gas in my house ever again.

Electricity may be more expensive but what price your life?

All these kinds of events help you to realise that life is fleeting, and moreover that it changes continuously.

We are not guaranteed tomorrow or even this afternoon, and we should live life to the full for as long as we are able to.

Another two acquaintances of mine died, one in a car accident another of a heart attack although quite young.

It was quite a year.

CHAPTER 9- BECOMING A TEACHER

As ever life went on and I was running out of money. I had invested some of it on an intensive course for the peseta equivalent of 500 euros. It was a good investment not only for learning Spanish but also that I did end up working at that academy in Torrevieja later on.

At that time, I was doing anything and everything to bring money in and keep afloat. Airport runs, babysitting, cleaning etc. The easiest work to get in this area is of course in the bars or restaurants, but I could not do that as I had my now nearly 2 years old son to think about.

He was at nursery, which was a very reasonable price compared to the UK, but of course only daytime. I saw an advert for a native English teacher in San Juan, Alicante a couple of early evenings a week. I applied and was accepted.

It was miles away, an hour and a half drive, and the few hours a week I worked only just covered the petrol really. However, I needed experience, and this was the first teaching job I was offered.

I remember vividly the first class I taught. I was just shown into a classroom, hands a board pen and the kids marched in. No planning, no advice about what level they were, and there were a lot of them. I was terrified.

Anyway, it must have gone well as I was invited to continue. I worked there a couple of months, and then with my updated CV I applied at the academy on Torrevieja where I had done my Intensive Spanish course and got the job.

The whole interview was in Spanish.

I just agreed to everything- but I certainly did not understand everything. I was offered the job.

When I came out to my car after the interview, it had disappeared. This was my first experience with the mysterious parking rules in Spain.

If you park where seems to be fine and you could be towed away, if you park where you are not too sure, you are normally fine.

My new boss helped me track down my car which had been taken to the pound. 80 euros thank you very much.

In Spain you are charged for the towing away and each hour in the pound, so you better hope you find out where it is quickly.

If you are not sure if a parking space is ok or not look at the pavement at the side. If it isn't you will see traces of stickers left for previous unfortunate souls who have had their vehicles removed.

Although Torrevieja is much closer than San Juan distance wise, it took me nearly as long to get to work due to the traffic and the difficulty parking, especially in the summer.

Torrevieja is unbearable then, it is unbelievably busy. This also applies to Easter or any other holiday time, when all the "madrileños" arrive at their holiday homes and take over the town.

One of the most unbelievable things I have seen was one recent Easter time when I had to reluctantly go into Torrevieja.

It was even busier than usual as it was market day, and I had my son´s German Shepherd dog in the back of my car. It was quite a warm day, but I know I would just be popping out of the car for a moment, and she would be fine. As long as the car was moving it was perfectly cool.

Suddenly, right in the centre of Torrevieja near the "Estación de Autobuses" (the Bus Station), we hit a traffic jam. The cars were gridlocked.

A bus was trying to leave the bus station, but a car had parked badly on the corner and the bus could not swing around it. In typical Spanish fashion, horns were blaring, and people were out of their cars gesticulating and shouting, but the owner of the car did not appear.

It seemed to go on forever, and I was worrying about my son´s dog that was starting to pant. Where were the police to tow the car away when you needed it? They had taken mine away quickly enough when I was being interviewed. This car was parked in a much worse place and was actually causing an obstruction.

Just as it seemed we would be there forever an amazing thing happened. Approximately 20 guys appeared out of nowhere and approached the offending car. To my total amazement, they positioned themselves around the car and lifted it up and placed it on the pavement, to give the bus room to swing around.

This worked, unbelievably. The bus JUST had enough space. There was a nail-biting moment when the front of the bus passed within millimetres of a shop window, but miraculously it just managed to turn with no damage done.

The jam eased, and we were able to complete our mission. This is a prime example of the difference between Spain and the UK. I do not thing that would ever have happened there.

Anyway, back to my story. I was working in the Academy in Torrevieja for approximately 2.50 euros per hour. I was doing everything I was asked to. Teaching English, reception, cleaning.

That is when I discovered that in Spain the wages are terrible. A contract is like gold dust and most Spanish people will endure low wages as long as they receive some sort of contract, so they have their Social Security paid. That way they receive free health care and contribute toward a pension. Also should they lose their job they will receive "finikitos" (a payoff from the employer", and be entitled to "Paro"- unemployment benefit.

Many people (as I was) are on part-time contracts but work full time. It is very expensive for an employer to take someone on a full-time contract, so they do not tend to do it.

However, part of my package was to participate in several Spanish courses so that was very useful, as I really was on a mission to learn Spanish. Also, I had to speak Spanish every day with the other people who worked there, so I did improve quite quickly with the combination of the classes and the daily speaking and listening practice.

Another thing that helped immensely was teaching English. My students were mostly Spanish and like to have things explained to them in Spanish. Grammar etc. I started to advance quite quickly during the 2 years I worked there. I was also watching Spanish television and children's films and videos (pre-DVD or Netflix days!!) with my son. I read him goodnight stories and helped him with his homework.

The hardest thing for me was listening. I got to a stage where I was ok in conversation with one person but got a bit lost when in a group. I would always get the joke a couple of seconds after everyone else, and it took a lot of concentration to keep up.

One person I worked with was a man called José. He was from Andalucía, and I never felt that he liked me very much. His accent was virtually impossible to decipher, and it seemed to me that he deliberately spoke quickly so I would struggle to understand. Many times, I had no clue what he was saying, and I would just smile and say "si".

One morning I came into work, and he was the first person I saw.

- "Buenos días, ¿qué tal?" I said.

He replied:

- "Muy bien, porque hoy no tengo la regla".

For those of you who do not understand Spanish, this translates to:

"Very good, because today I don´t have my period."

I took a step back, and repeated it to him, and he realised that I had, maybe for the first time, understood exactly what he was saying. God knows what he had been saying to me all that time.

He was so apologetic, and from that day on he treated me with much more respect and eventually we did become friends.

That was a turning point for me with my Spanish.

The courses taught at that Academy were Immersion Courses, that is only Spanish was spoken, even for beginners. This worked well for me, as I had only just completed my degree course only a year earlier and my brain was still in studying mode. However later when I started teaching Spanish, I did discover that many things I had thought that I understood, in fact I had not. The lack of an explanation in my language meant that I had often got the wrong idea about certain things.

For other people, long out of education, this method was practically impossible, especially for beginners. I noticed that many British people started the course with enthusiasm but gave up after just a couple of days, quite a high percentage of them. This academy offered Spanish classes for German people with explanations in German, and I suggested to my boss that she should think about maybe doing the same for English speakers, with explanations in English. She rubbished the idea, saying that it was not necessary, the English speakers were quite happy with only Spanish spoken.

Ok then.

These students may not have kicked up a fuss, but they would certainly have gone off and told everyone they know that the course was rubbish.

This is the reason that 2 years after working for a pittance at this school and finally starting to teach Spanish myself. I promoted the fact that my Spanish classes were explained in English. I now have students of all different nationalities but one thing they have in common is that they speak English, and they like to have the grammar explained to them in a language that they understand.

English, Scottish, Welsh, Irish, Swedish, Danish, Faroese, Dutch, German, French, Belgian, American, Norwegian, Icelandic, Russian, Polish, New Zealanders, Rumanian- they have all passed through the doors of my classroom. Apologies if I have missed any nationality!!

CHAPTER 10 – A TERRIBLE EVENT AND HOW IT ALL STARTED

It was while I was working at this Academy that I suffered another significant loss.

One morning I was on my morning break and the receptionist Toni told me that my brother Simon had rang. She had told him that I was in class, and did he want to leave a message.

He had declined and said he would call back later. I thought it was strange, but I did not have time to call him back just then.

Later that afternoon he called again, and I was there. His exact words were: -

- "Dad died this morning"

I literally threw the telephone down and ran into an empty room screaming. I just could not compute what I was hearing. My Dad, as do most dads, just always seemed so strong, so invincible, I could not believe that he was gone.

My mum had been in bad health for a while and was suffering with dementia. I knew that my Dad was struggling in caring for her. As I was in Spain, one very good thing that I do have are many lovely letters from him, that I would not have had otherwise.

Although he was not a very emotionally demonstrative person, in his letters he had been able to be much more affectionate than he ever was in person.

My poor Dad had gone to bed the night before and had simply not woken up.

I could imagine him not wanting to go, and being lifted from the bed by some higher power, it was time for him to rest now.

My poor Mum had found him, and the neighbours had found her wandering up and down the road looking for help. My Dad was a very proud and independent man, he would not ask for help and the stress of caring for my mum had ultimately proven to be too much.

God bless my Daddy.

I went back to the UK for the funeral, and I went to see him in the chapel of rest.

He did look peaceful. He looked so tiny though.

After the funeral, I briefly considered staying in the UK to look after my mum, but it just wasn´t possible as my son was only 2 years old at the time. Even that week I spent there looking after her was difficult.

My Mum died a few years later, one of my sisters, Susan luckily was able to care for her.

My Mum was quite far gone with dementia by then and had a series of strokes, her death was sad but almost a relief as she too now was at peace, her and my Dad together again.

They had been married over 50 years.

Although it had not all been plain sailing, they had come through their problems, had 5 children, 12 grandchildren, and several great grandchildren.

I came back to Spain and would only see my Mum alive once more after that.

So, I was working for a pittance at this school in Torrevieja, really struggling to make ends meet. A friend of mine (who I was later to enter another disastrous relationship with, I can really pick them) told me of a job he had seen advertised in Villa Martin Plaza. It was a holiday rental agency, and they were looking for someone who could speak English and Spanish.

My Spanish was not perfect, but I could cope in most situations, so I went for an interview, and I got the job.

I was so happy; it was much closer to where I lived.

The hourly rate was more like 5 euros an hour than 2.50, and a full-time contract was included in the package.

It all seemed great.

During the three months I worked there I discovered that in Spain jobs that look promising are not what they appear. Maybe it was a better wage than the Academy and a full- time contract, but oh my gosh they wanted blood. As I left the Academy my boss did warn me that employment in Spain was not always what it appeared. She also kindly told me that if it didn´t work out, my job with her would be waiting for me.

The rental agency was run by a bigger company, but the manager of my branch was a British woman who to be frank I discovered was pretty much unhinged.

I was on call practically 24 hours to meet people with keys or welcome packs. My official hours were forty, but I was basically working double that. I had to use my own car and petrol and never received any compensation for that. They kept promising it but it never materialised.

Then after my three-month contract finished, they did not renew it. I discovered that this was what they always did, to avoid ever having to give anyone an indefinite contract where you have so many more employment rights.

I was without work with my son to support and I just did not know what to do.

I know that I could return to the Torrevieja Academy, but the wages were so low I just could not make ends meet there.

At the time, a friend of mine was on holiday visiting me, Christine. Christine was a photographer who had recently decided to become self- employed, and it was working out for her. The story of what happened then is told in one of the blogs at the end of this book, so I will not repeat it here. Enough to say I was terrified of being self-employed, no one at that point in my family had ever done it and it just was so alien to my working-class roots.

I started teaching for myself, twice I left this employment and tried something else, and twice they had disastrous consequences. These are the two experiences I will relate now.

CHAPTER 11- ON THE RADIO

At first my little school was doing so well, getting busier and busier. This was the boom of the early 2000´s and new people were coming to live here daily. This time not only people retiring here, but families coming to give their children a better life. They were good times, but of course all booms bust in the end.

I was renting a local that was costing me 800 euros a month. I could not pay it anymore, so I moved everything to the basement of my home and started doing the classes there instead. This was of course pre-Zoom days; classes could only be done in person.

It was ok, I was just about earning enough, but I had to let my receptionist and other teacher go.

One day I saw an advertisement for a salesperson for a local radio station. I applied, thinking I could fit that in with the classes I had. It was commission only, car and telephone supplied, and this suited me fine. I was the only person there who spoke Spanish, so I was able to deal with all their Spanish clients. I built up my client base and was soon earning very good commissions.

There was so much bitchiness there though.

The sales manager seemed to hate everyone, including her own sister who also worked there. She was one of those women who appears all sweetness and light, but in fact is granite bitch. She created a nasty atmosphere of gossip and Chinese whispers.

I cannot bear two-faced people; I prefer someone who openly does not like me than someone who pretends to but really doesn´t. The day she told me about her sister having an abortion was the day I realised that is she was so nasty about her own sister, I basically had no chance.

Also, I had worked for myself long enough that I dd not like being ordered around, especially by fools. It worked well for a while as I was left to my own devices- as no one else could speak Spanish anyway.

However, inevitably, an argument ensued, and I was asked to come in and talk about it. At that meeting they confiscated my phone and car keys; told me I was sacked and drove me home.

That awful sales manager tried to say she was "sorry" and it was all I could do to not tell her exactly what I thought of her. I had run down all my classes down as I gradually was working more and more for the radio station, and I had to start all over again. This would not be the last time that I would have to do this.

Difficult times. When I look back a lot of my life in Spain has been difficult, mainly financially.

It is so difficult to find regular, decently paid work, which is why so many people work for themselves and have their fingers in so many pies.

I answered another advertisement for a salesperson, this time for a newspaper.

My time in sales has made me so much more sympathetic to those who do this difficult job. You are normally on commission only and you are often paying your own petrol and using your own car, computer and telephone.

So please be kind to anyone who tries to sell you advertising. ?

Cold- calling is part if the job, and it is so difficult. I hated it. However, I had to earn money somehow.

I could not work in a bar or restaurant as my son was still young and I could not work evenings. I started doing some classes again and just lurched along from week to week.

One day we attended an exhibition and that's where the next chapter of my story started.

CHAPTER 12- 1CAR1

At the exhibition was a UK car hire company. Their purpose of advertising in Spain was that when people returned to the UK for holidays to visit the family, they would often need to hire a car. Their base office was in Leeds, and they would come out not only to Spain but to other Ex-Pat enclaves to promote. I got chatting to the guy there, Matthew, and he kindly took out some advertising with our newspaper.

We were in touch, and as time went on he asked me if I was interested in a full-time position as their representative in Spain. He had been thinking about taking someone on for a long time but had not met the right person.

This was like a miracle to me. Of course, I was interested. A regular income, a telephone, a car. A "normal" job.

He invited me over to Leeds for an interview and I borrowed the money to go over, as I was absolutely living on the edge at that time.

I started working for them and I have to say that I loved that job.

Talking to people and promotion is what I am good at, just not cold calling. The job consisted of sponsorship, generally promoting the name of 1Car1 to the Ex pat Community.

Once again, I stopped my classes as this was a full-time job and I could not do both. Sometimes I had to work weekends etc, but I didn´t really mind as it was a good job, and I was hoping to have time off the following summer when everything goes so quiet in Spain.

That Christmas I had my first paid time off since I came to Spain 10 years earlier.

One thing I remember especially vividly was a speech I had to make at an awards ceremony. I had to make the speech in both English and Spanish in front of over 500 people. I was terrified. As I spoke, my heart was hammering in my chest, and I had visions of having a heart attack and an ambulance having to be called. However, I got through it, and I can honestly say I have never feared speaking in public since.

The Spanish side of business improved, and bookings were up. I found us a new office (the previous one had been found by another contact and was not good). I took on a part-time member of staff and the training manager came over to train her.

Then suddenly one day, totally without warning, an email message came through the company system telling us all that the Company was going into administration and our salary due at the end of that month could not be guaranteed. What a bombshell.

I had to just pack everything up, leave the office and deal with everything here in Spain for no money. I was totally cut off as I was not in the Head Office and once more, start over from scratch. I had no income whatsoever and no savings.

This time it was the credit crunch that had taken its toll on 1CAR1, though I find it difficult to believe that the owners had no idea whatsoever that it was coming.

I do not regret working for 1CAR1, as I acquired many contacts and had many nice experiences with them. Also, the friendship I now have with my boss Matthew and his wife Cherie is so valuable to me.

I have even taught their daughter Abigail Spanish; she was born that awful year so that was a very stressful time for them also. In fact, anyone who worked at 1CAR1.

As I am writing this, I find it difficult to believe that I am even still here and surviving. Maybe life would have been easier if I had stayed in the UK, but of course there is no guarantee of this.

Once again, I had to build up my classes from scratch, and I came to believe that I was fated to be a Spanish teacher. Everything else I had tried had gone completely wrong. As I was saying earlier, I do believe that things happen for a reason. Sometimes it is some time before we know why.

I started a database, one thing I did have from 1CAR1 were many email addresses. Maybe you will feel it was the wrong thing to do to use this to start promoting my Spanish classes again, but if so you have probably never been in a situation where you were so desperate.

Gradually, “poco a poco” I began to fill my classes again.

I began to do Intensive Courses, and these proved popular with people who wanted to learn Spanish quickly. From these classes I developed a manual, and from the manual gradually emerged my first book- Break the Language Barrier Level 1.

Of course, this would never have happened had those other jobs worked out. I have been gently pushed in the direction that I am going, for whatever reason.

Level 1 was followed by Level 2, then Level 3, then Level 4. Any of you that have progressed through those books (thank you by the way) will have noticed that in Level 4 there are a few mistakes.

I have to admit I was pretty "booked out" by then. I have also produced a couple of dual language story books and I have several more in mind.

Recently I released the Break the Language barrier Level 1 for Spanish people wanting to learn English, and a Level 2 is in the pipeline.

Then there is if course this book.

I hope you have enjoyed it and not found it too "whiny" or traumatic.

I have faced a lot of challenges on my Spanish journey, but I know so many other people have faced much more challenges than I.

What I did not know 6 years ago was that I was about to face my biggest challenge yet. One that would very nearly sweep me away and everything I cared about. One that I would not wish on my very worst enemy and that I know, and still know, is a common problem people face… I am not ready yet to publicly discuss this, maybe in the next one.

So that is my story of how I came to live in Spain. I hope you enjoyed reading it and that I have not offended anyone. The rest of this book consists of some of my experiences whilst living here, mainly in a work environment.

These are stories taken from my blog, Confessions of a Spanish Teacher, they are all 100% true.

Thank you for reading, I appreciate every one of you that has taken this time to spend with me.

See you in the next one ⍰

CHAPTER 13-SPANISH TEACHER OR AGONY AUNT?

It was amazing how quickly the classes built up...

Anyone who has ever lived in an Ex-Pat community will know how small it is.

For every one student I acquired I acquired at least one more.

Friends, family, neighbours... This was before the advent of social media or even the internet. In those days in my part of Spain we didn't even have proper phones, just radio ones that hardly ever worked. Mobiles were just becoming popular but there were very few reception masts around, so coverage was sketchy to say the least. I normally could get a signal by hanging off the roof terrace with a following wind though.

Word of mouth and recommendation was the best way of attracting new students, along with my advert in the Television Magazine. Everyone read that, we Brits like our telly.

One day I received a call from a lady called Carol to go and give classes at the home in a town up the road- She had come to Spain with her much older husband Alan and she already had a good level of Spanish.

When we come to live in a foreign country, we leave a lot of our social network behind. Friends, family, work. Many couples find they can't stand the sight of each other after a few months thrown together with no distractions and there are many infidelities and breakups.

In the intimacy of their home, people often start to treat their Spanish class as more of a counselling session than a class. This is what happened with Carol as she began increasingly to relate her marital problems to me in Spanish.

The awkward thing was is that this normally took place in the kitchen as her hapless non-Spanish speaking husband made us cups of tea and asked if we were okay.

I squirmed as she gave me intimate details of her affair with a Spaniard she had met in Benidorm whilst Alan passed me the biscuits. She went on to tell me how she was going to leave Alan soon and how he couldn't perform in the bedroom as I tried to keep a poker face and smile politely at him accepting a custard cream, trying desperately not to form a mental picture.

Eventually Carol left poor Alan and went to live with her Spanish lover. She didn't need Spanish classes any more... or counselling ...

Alan contacted me looking for Spanish classes, but I politely declined, claiming my timetable was full. I think he just wanted a shoulder to cry on but hey, don't we all.

But being an agony aunt was easy compared to dealing with exhibitionists and alcoholics on their home turf!! More to follow....

CHAPTER 14- DRUNKEN SPANISH/ ESPAÑOL BORRACHO

Carl and Mary are lovely people.

So nice, friendly, would do anything for you and were keen to learn Spanish.

We arranged classes and I started going to their flat twice a week.

The flat was only six months old, a new build from the building explosion here in Spain. I realised quite quickly that absolutely NO cleaning had been done in that flat during those 6 months. I felt I had stepped into an episode of one of those extreme clean reality shows.

I am by no means housewife of the year material as anyone who knows me will tell you, but there is untidy and there is **DIRTY**. And then there is **FILTHY**...

"Excuse the mess", they said, "we did have a cleaner, but she only came once for some reason and we can´t seem to get hold of her".

Poor woman.

They had two dogs, beautiful dogs, but it was obvious they were allowed to poo and wee in the flat and it was not always cleaned up immediately.

The toilet was something else, I made the mistake of going the first day and spent the rest of the class trying not to gag whilst teaching the alphabet and pronunciation. From then on, I made sure I never needed to go again whilst I was there.

Carl and Mary were always offering tea and coffee, biscuits, even lunch. They must have wondered why I never lost weight whilst teaching them Spanish as being on a diet was the only excuse I could come up with as they tried to press them on me.

But the worse day came when I turned up at the flat one day at 11.00 a.m. for class as arranged and they were not only clearly drunk, but it also seemed they had had an argument.

I offered to return another day when they were more receptive, but Carl insisted that I carried on with the class as normal.

I was stuck there for an hour trying to explain "ser" and "estar" to a very drunken, belligerent couple in a filthy house.

Anyone who has ever tried to understand these two verbs to be in Spanish will know how difficult that was!!

I still have these nightmarish flashbacks of being pinned down on the sofa between them as they glared at each other and breathed beer and cigarette fumes over me.

Carl asked ridiculous questions with alcohol glazed eyes. I couldn't even escape to the loo as I was terrified what that would be like.

Luckily eventually I managed to extricate myself and I never had to go back there again. It was this mainly this experience and the next one I will relate regarding the exhibitionist that decided me it was time to find some premises to teach rather than go into people's homes where I just never knew quite what would happen ....

CHAPTER 15-SPANISH IN A THONG/ ESPAÑOL EN UNA TANGA

Another enduring traumatic memory I have of teaching Spanish in people's home is "thong-gate".

No, not me in a thong you will be glad to hear.

Personally, I have always thought thongs were uncomfortable and hideous and don't look good on anyone unless they have a flawless body, especially men. (sorry)

One day I had the unfortunate experience of finding this to definitely be true...

Thong in Spanish is "tanga" and I was definitely tanga-ed that day.

Karen was a nice enough lady who I had been teaching Spanish to for several weeks over the winter in her home. I had also had the dubious pleasure of taking her husband Billy to the hospital a couple of times as his interpreter.

Interpreting is another source of interesting experiences I will be looking at in this blog. I didn't like him much, he was arrogant and nasty, and to all accounts he wasn´t averse to laying hands on Karen when he had had a drink.

Alcohol is a bit problem in the Ex-Pat community in Spain.

It is cheap, the sun is normally shining, and most of us tend to drink more here than in the UK.

As winter changed to spring the temperatures increased and I went around there one beautiful morning and Karen suggested we take class on the patio as it was so nice. I agreed, and all was well until about fifteen minutes in when Billy suddenly appeared and walked past us to go and lie by the pool, and guess what he was wearing?

And a very small one at that. It left absolutely nothing to the imagination.

At first I thought:

-"Poor guy, he will be mortified, he must not have realised that I was here".

After the 5th or 6th time he walked past in so many minutes it suddenly dawned on me that it was possible it might be **because** I was there.

I looked beseechingly at Karen, but she totally ignored him and just concentrated on her worksheet.

Seated and trapped on the **very** small patio, I was at eye level with Billy´s budgie smugglers every time he walked past, and was regaled with a lovely back view as he went past to the pool.

I wouldn´t have liked it even if he was a Chippendale, and Billy wasn´t ....

He was at least 65 years old, and he was thin, and I mean thin, almost emaciated, with the leathery brown skin you get if you sunbathe too much here.

From the back his rear looked he like two conkers rubbing together.

Thank God the class was only an hour long, because those last 45 minutes went very, very slowly.

Billy pranced backwards and forward and stopped to chat often directly in front of me. It was horrible.

To this day I cannot see a thong without a shudder going through me.

I must add here that most people I have taught Spanish to in their homes have been lovely and very welcoming, and have not worn thongs or been drunk :)

However, these bad experiences I did have, along with the fact I was getting busier and running out of time to drive from one student to another, meant I decided to find some premises to teach Spanish from.

I did not have to go through this again. That is where Charlie.com came in and I will be talking about that soon.

But the next couple of "confessions" will be from some notable experiences I had as an interpreter many years ago.

CHAPTER 16-MÉDICOS Y PRESERVATIVOS / DOCTORS AND CONDOMS

When I first came to my part of Spain 20 years ago, it was largely undiscovered by British tourists, and my little village was even smaller than it is now. There were only approximately 1,500 people on the electoral roll.

It was in fact bigger than that as many foreigners lived here in the surrounding "urbanizations'" but were largely unregistered in those days.

Later the building boom and the growing awareness and massive influx of "guiris", (foreigners) would change this.

In those days the local Health Centre here was ran by two "old school" doctors.

I got to know one of them, Doctor Garcia, quite well as I was offering an interpreter service and I took many people to see him.

So many that he even started to take me out on his house calls if they were British, though looking back this was probably against the rules.

He had a lovely dead pan sense of humour, and as an interpreter true to my word I had to repeat many a strange question to him, to which he would simply arch an eyebrow and reply expressionlessly.

I think many "more mature" people then simply didn't realise that Spain was not a Third World Country and indeed you **were** given hospital meals and they **did** have modern technology not use leeches on you to cure everything.

I think the most memorable appointment for me was the day I took Doris. Doris was well into her 70's if not 80's, and her husband Gerry the same.

One thing I have learned about medical interpreting is that often during the consultation you almost become invisible and part of the scenery like a nurse.

People, male or female, happily strip off in front of you without drawing the curtain and of course they must tell you all the gory details of their condition.

Part of the reason I was so determined to learn Spanish when I came here was that I did not want to ever have to go to the doctors for a personal type of illness and be forced to relate it through a third party.

Doris´s problem was quite personal. She related it to me while we sat waiting to be called.

Sexual intercourse with Gerry had become a little uncomfortable and could be followed by mild blood spotting …

Ok.

In we went and I related Doris´s problem to Doctor Garcia.

I was embarrassed and blushing, but Doris was totally unfazed:

-"Tell him as well, I have no idea why this is happening because my husband Gerry is not very big..."

I duly reported what she had asked, and Dr Garcia's face was impassive.

The recommended treatment was KY Jelly and some special condoms.

I explained this to Doris and her last question was:

-"Ask him who puts the condom on, me or Gerry?"

This time Dr Garcia's mouth did twitch a little, as he looked me directly in the eye and said:

-"Tell her... love is a beautiful thing and a matter for two people...

The person to put it on should be whomever seems natural at the time...."

Classic... and very good advice.

CHAPTER 17- GYNECOLOGY SPANISH STYLE/ GINECOLGOGÍA ESPAÑOLA

Spain is a world leader in many medical procedures.

I think many people who have had treatment here would agree that if you have to be ill anywhere, you have a better chance of recovery in Spain than in many places.

For medical care, you would be struggling to complain, but unfortunately for the "TLC" or tender loving care factor along with bedside manner maybe not...

Friends and family are expected to do that, medical care is exemplary but that is as far as it goes.

Another thing that has become apparent to me over years of interpreting and personal and family use of the Health Service here in Spain is that privacy and personal dignity is not always respected.

Doors are often left open while examinations take place, allowing people sitting outside to gawp in. If the door is closed, staff often enter and leave the room without knocking, or consultants have inappropriate conversations with colleagues over the heads of patients. These are all things I have seen many times.

But I think the worst thing I saw was when I took Miriam to visit the gynaecologist.

Miriam was quite a timid lady, and I would imagine it was embarrassing enough to have to take a virtual stranger along to interpret at a very personal examination. At least I was a female, and I always was very discreet, but it must have been difficult for her still.

The Consultant was fortunately female also, and all went well as Miriam was required to undress from the waist down and lie down on the bed with her feet in the customary stirrups.

The Doctor donned a pair of latex gloves, and the examination began. She was asking questions that I was relaying to Miriam, and then back to the Doctor with the answers. The Doctors right hand was fully inserted in Miriam´s private area.

Suddenly, a phone rang…

It was the Doctors mobile which was on the desk next to the table.

The Doctor looked at it to see who was calling...

I figured it must be something very urgent as, incredibly, the doctor slowly extricated her hand from Miriam`s fandango and gingerly picked up the mobile, without removing the latex gloves she was wearing.

Holding it with fingertips only, she pressed the button, and held it precariously to her ear.

-"Hola hijo"- she said, which to those of you who don' t know means "hello son".

A five-minute long conversation ensued which dealt mainly with what she was going to collect from the supermarket on the way home to cook for lunch... Maybe not quite as urgent as I had assumed...

During this time poor Miriam lay legs akimbo and I tried to look anywhere else in the room.

Lunch menu sorted, the Consultant replaced the phone on the table, reinserted her right hand into

Miriam’ s private area, and completed the examination.

I just presume and hope she did get a baby wipe or something similar to clean the mobile later...

CHAPTER 18- 50 SHADES OF SPANISH / 50 SOMBRAS DE ESPAÑOL

Being a Spanish teacher, or probably any kind of teacher, attracts admirers.

I am not vain enough to think it is my stunning good looks or sparkling personality, just a kind of teacher/student fantasy that many men harbour from schooldays. They make jokes about detentions and canes and punishments as if no one has ever made them before. As I teach mainly adults, this has caused problems at times over the 20 years I have been teaching. Some have been more welcome than others.

These sorts of men are normally married or in a relationship, and usually I'm afraid not the sort of man that my fantasies are made of, but this doesn't seem to bother them.

They normally come with partners who think they are some kind of love god, and any woman would consider herself lucky to be propositioned by them, therefore it must the "lucky" woman's fault if their man is lead astray.

Hmm, have never really understood that. Personally, I find it awkward and insulting,

One very unwelcome one was Charlie. Charlie was married to Christine. He hadn't even been for classes yet when he took a shine to me.

As we had mutual friends, we were occasionally in social situations together. He was a nice enough guy but about as far removed from Brad Pitt or Idris Elba, my own personal fantasy men, as you could imagine.

It started with uncomfortable staring, then threats to come for Spanish classes one day, as if that was all I was really waiting for in my life. I must give off some very strange signals as I swear that I do not remember flirting with this guy in any way shape or form.

It came to a head one night at a party. It started as we were all having drinks and I had to walk past him. "Oh sorry" I apologised as I thought I had accidentally brushed his hand with my backside as I walked past.

I soon realised as his hand then continued to give my "culo" a massage this had not quite been the case.

When situations like this happen, what you really want to do is slap them across the face and deliver a few choice words. What you end up doing normally is nothing, because you don´t want to cause a scene and their wife and all your friends are right there...

As we all sat in the restaurant eating it was worse.

Every time I looked up; he was staring at me intently with quite a scary leering expression. I got up to go to the toilet and he followed me and whispered in my ear "I´ll be coming for Spanish classes soon".

Again, like it was some tantalizing secret we shared, but unfortunately, I wasn't quite in on it. I just smiled weakly. I knew I was supposed to feel privileged about this in some way but somehow, I just was not feeling it.

Was I missing something?

After the meal we went to another bar and I just tried to keep away from him, as the alcohol was flowing, and I knew this was likely to:

A. increase the chances of him doing something else, and

B. increase the chances of me punching him in the face.

Deciding I did not want either of these to happen, and aware that his wife Christine, was jealously watching every more he made, I simply kept my distance.

All seemed uneventful until home time. I was chatting with a friend when suddenly he appeared at my ear, taking advantage of the fact his wife was distracted for a moment saying goodbye to someone else. He leant over with that same intent, leering expression he had been wearing all night and whispered slowly:

“Just imagine being tied up, blindfolded and licked all over...”

My jaw dropped open and all I could manage to say weakly was

“Er… what?”

At that moment I was saved as Christine appeared and practically dragged him off by the ear making some comment to me that I don´t even want to repeat.

As a friend commented later, maybe due to fact I would have been wearing a blindfold, it would not have been so bad.....??

Charlie did eventually come for classes and in fact behaved impeccably, so luckily, I never actually got to find out.

CHAPTER 19- THE WIDOWER/ EL VIUDO

Being a Spanish teacher influences your social life.

When you go out in company of Ex- Pats and they find out you teach Spanish they do one of two things.

They may become defensive and obviously uncomfortable about their own level of Spanish as they have maybe lived here for years and never bothered trying to learn.

Failing that, if they are keen to learn they therefore start speaking to me in Spanish wanting to take the rare opportunity to practice what they have learned.

Unfortunately, although they live in Spain they probably live in an area inhabited by Ex Pats and rarely use it, which is a shame.

However, I prefer the first kind for a couple of reasons.

Firstly, if I am not working, I do not really want to speak in Spanish as I am relaxing, and no one wants to be reminded of work in their spare time. I sympathise with doctors who go to parties and are shown rashes or asked what this or that pain means as soon as they divulge what they do.

Secondly if I am out and drinking, I am the opposite of my students who normally say after a drink or two they have more confidence and feel more relaxed in speaking.

For me is the contrary. After a few drinks and I start to relax I have no interest in speaking Spanish (unless with Spaniards of course), I just want to socialise without thinking too hard.

Also, I feel that I can never really let my hair down when people know I am a teacher, I always feel I should behave in a certain way especially if I bump into parents of students!

As the Ex-Pat community is a small one here I very often encounter students past and present when I am out, and when it is the early hours of the morning in some late night bar I can only hope they are letting their hair down too.

This is how I “met” the widower Michael again.

Michael had been a student of mine a couple of years earlier along with his wife Tina. He had not done many classes, she had stayed longer, as he was working and many times, he could not make it.

I remembered him particularly as he was an attractive guy but I also remembered that his wife was a very nice woman.

So, there I was, approximately 2 a.m. in a late bar after many vodkas and quite drunk.

I didn't even see him coming, but suddenly he was by my side at the bar fixing me with the stare I remembered unsettling me so much in class.

Luckily, he was drunk too.

"Hello. Do you remember me". He was from Northern Ireland, and he rasped the question in that deep sultry voice all the men from there seem to have.

- "Yes of course. It´s Michael isn´t it?"

I answered, trying to put on my sensible head and actually put a coherent sentence together.

- “How´s your wife?”

I cast through the vodka fog for her name but couldn´t get it, I was just trying to make some polite conversation and not let slip I was in fact extremely drunk.

Not at all appropriate for a teacher.

“She´s dead...”

Ah. Shit….

A couple of excruciating minutes followed while I wondered what the hell to say next...

“Ah I´m sorry. What happened?” was the pathetic question I managed.

“Cancer...”

Double shit...

I really wanted the floor to open and swallow me.

Maybe it helped us both being drunk as we did move on from that and we started to go out together for many months.

I really liked Michael but unfortunately, I did get to understand where the phrase the Merry Widower comes from as it transpired that Michael was in fact seeing several women to help him recover from losing poor Tina.

Ah well, the one that got away- again

CHAPTER 20- MERRY CHRISTMAS/ FELÍZ NAVIDAD!!!!

Christmas is quite different here in Spain, certainly from the UK. As the main Spanish holiday is in fact the Epiphany, on the 6th January. The Three Kings arrive the evening before and dispense the gifts, rather than "Papa Noel" on the Eve of the 25th.

When I first came here 20 years ago in this area you would not have even known it was Christmas, as there was absolutely no hype or build up. Now the influx of the Ex Pats and their influence have changed it somewhat, but it is still very quiet and civilised around the shops and supermarkets, except maybe the British supermarkets.

I have never really understood why so much food is bought when the shops are only in fact closed for one day.

In one way I miss the atmosphere, but in another it is nice to be able to go quietly to the Shopping Centre and the supermarkets right up to Christmas Eve, without the massive number of shoppers and the fights over the last bag of parsnips.

On the minus side, sometimes it does seem interminable,

The fiestas seem to go on forever after Christmas day with New Year's Eve (Nochevieja- Old night) a week later and then of course The Three Kings (Los Reyes Magos) another week after that!

In Spain Christmas Eve (Nochebuena-Good Night) is when the family get together and exchange any gifts. Restaurants are rarely open as this is important family time for everyone, these banquets normally take place in the home of a family member.

The feast is a sumptuous dinner of many courses including a lot of seafood, that starts at 10 or even 11 pm and goes on into the early hours of the morning. Christmas day itself is very insignificant and Boxing Day does not exist here, it is a normal working day.

In the run up to the last day of classes before Christmas, I have traditionally offered my students chocolate with their tea or coffee, and a Spanish liqueur of some description.

"Ponche" (a brandy based liqueur) or "crema de orujo", (a kind of Baileys type liqueur using "oruja" a Spanish liqueur instead of whisky) and just as yummy.

One year attending classes that week were Olga, a Russian lady, and her husband Selwyn who is Welsh.

Olga appeared to be the boss in the relationship, and I did think she did not look very happy when he accepted a glass of Ponche with his "café con leche". However he took one anyway and it did go down quite quickly I noticed.

5 minutes later Selwyn was beetroot red and gasping for breath clutching his chest!!!

“He is not supposed to drink” Olga muttered, “he recently had a heart attack and can´t have any stimulants”

Why do people not tell me these things before?

I was seriously thinking that I may have my first ever death in class and was wondering if it would be considered my fault as I gave him the bloody Ponche, and I offered to ring an ambulance.

“No” said Olga, “He will be fine- Take your inhaler Selwyn!!”

He did not look fine to me, I have never seen anyone so red as that, but Selwyn did as he was told and took his inhaler and went out for some fresh air. Slowly but surely, he returned to normal.

Phew!!

CHAPTER 21- EL PRINCIPE CENTRE IS BORN WITH CHARLIE.COM/ NACÍO EL PRINCIPE CENTRE CON CHARLIE.COM.

This part of Spain in the late nineties was a bit of a communications black spot. The internet was yet to arrive, and in fact you would struggle to make even a phone call as mobile masts were few and far between and functioning land lines were like gold dust. Most people had a kind of radio phone in the house that only worked with a following wind and if there was an "r" in the month.

People got together mainly in bars and if you wanted to talk to people that was where you had to go to find them. When Charlie arrived in my area from the UK, he was a bit of an enigma as he knew about computers!!!

He quickly earned the nickname Charlie.com for this very reason.

He started to come for Spanish classes in my home and he took me out a couple of times, but only as a friend, and we got chatting.

I told him that I was a bit fed up of teaching in people's houses and in my house, and had seen a "local"- (office space) available for rent that I thought was suitable for a language school.

I was a very poor single parent just trying to earn a living in a country where doing just that is notoriously difficult. I just did not have the cash needed to set up a school, where I would have to pay advance rent and buy desks chairs etc and have a receptionist.

Charlie had money. I never really found out exactly where this money had come from, well it wasn`t my business anyway, and he was a dabbler. He didn't need to earn money, but he needed something to do, he was bored.

In the UK he had worked and worked, earned lots of money, and eventually had bought himself a fantastic big house. However, he said that when he went in and closed the door it was just an empty house as he had no family, so he had sold it up and come to Spain in search of something to occupy his time.

He wanted to set up an internet café, an absolute novelty here at the time. Most people did not have internet at home. He also planned to teach people how to use computers.

I took him to see the "local" I was interested in, and lo and behold we found out that it was in a place where internet was available. We decide to rent it together, he would invest the money needed to split it into two, furnish it, and I would pay him back my half bit by bit.

It was a very exciting and scary prospect at the same time. It meant "going legal", starting up a business that was registered with the Spanish tax and national insurance system.

It was situated in Urbanisation "Pueblo Principe" (Prince Town), hence the name was coined: "El Principe Centre" (The Prince Centre)

We did it, and opened our doors on the 1st May 2000. I already had many students from the classes I was doing in mine or other people's homes, and MOST of them came with me to the school.

Charlie.com set up his internet cafe and it was very popular with my students. Very soon we took on a receptionist between us and I got very busy.

However, things went wrong with Charlie.com in his Computer classes...

Charlie was a very intelligent guy but didn´t know how to teach... He assumed knowledge, a big no-no. Teaching is a gift that I believe you either have or you don´t. No amount of training or qualifications are going to give you the empathy you need with the student to be a good teacher.

The patience, the ability to smile through the most ridiculous question or repeat things a million times. To know when to correct, but not to destroy confidence, to just know what a student means with their question when nobody else understands what the hell they are talking about. And to never assume knowledge and be able to explain things in the most simplistic manner possible.

Charlie couldn´t do this. Most of his students, like mine, were older, possibly retired people who had perhaps never touched a computer in their whole lives. He couldn´t seem to understand that if you told someone to "right click twice on the mouse", they would not necessarily understand what you meant.

Firstly, they often did not even know what a mouse was, and secondly, they didn´t know how to right click it!!

At the end of the day, you have to start with the very basics and explain everything.

Charlie would say things like

- "What, you don`t know how to copy and paste? How have you even lived this long"

Ha ha.

Needless to say, this did not go down well with his paying customers.

Sometimes it is frustrating, but of course you can´t make the student feel like an idiot.

Often, I have come across people in my classes who have lived here for years and still don´t know what "café con leche", "gracias" or "por favor" means.

I can´t laugh and say-

"Oh my God, where have you been all these years?"

So, inevitably, Charlie's computer classes didn't work out and in December of the same year we opened Charlie told me he was bored and would not be coming back after the Christmas break.

From January I would have to pay all the expenses rent, electricity, phone, receptionist etc. myself.

That was a terrifying Christmas break for me as I didn't know if I could do it or not...

Charlie went on to meet a lady and settle down locally spending much of his time drunk in the local bars.

I hope he enjoyed it as he sadly passed away not long after with a brain tumor.

Charlie.com was irritating at times and could be difficult to work with but without him there never would have been an El Principe Centre...

CHAPTER 22- NIGHTMARE SUMMER SCHOOL/ PESADILLA DE LA ESCUELA DE VERANO

Things carried on, the school was busy enough and I was managing to pay the receptionist, the rent, electricity etc. However, summer was approaching, the first summer I was having to do this alone.

I was panicking as I knew that Spanish classes get very quiet in the summer due to the intense heat and that many of my students went back to their country for the summer, or had family out here to stay.

Unfortunately, my expenses did not reduce, so somehow, I had to think of a way to keep the cash flow consistent through this difficult period.

I came up with the idea of a summer school for children ages 5 to 16, to both learn Spanish and practice their English reading and writing.

Many British children that are brought up here in Spain, my own son included, know how to speak English but struggle to read or spell it, as they are in the Spanish state system and read and spell phonetically in the Spanish way.

So, I printed up some leaflets, set a price and a limit of 20 students divided into 2 classes, and took on a couple of temporary teachers to help out.

The places filled almost immediately, and we were ready to go for July and half of August. What could go wrong?

The first thing I want to say is that I have to give is a massive round of applause for any teacher in any normal school that has to deal with large class sizes and difficult children.

Actually, much more difficult than the children are the parents…

I came to realise that many parents look on any kind of school as a glorified babysitter, many of the parents of my students parked their kids and went off to spend the day in the pub.

They were no help whatsoever and in fact more of a hindrance in supporting any behavioural issue their kids might have. I learned that saying that “they have a few learning difficulties” could also be translated to “they are in fact a sociopath one step from borstal”

Also, I found that, despite repeatedly asking the parents to send in only healthy snacks and drinks, often it would be a bar of chocolate and a can of coke.

As if they weren't hyperactive enough.

Some were even sent in with money to "pop and get something from the bar downstairs".

Half a lager and a packet of pork scratchings? And who was supposed to accompany them when the teachers were occupied with the class?

Or were we supposed to let them go alone and just hope they weren't abducted?

We were too strict/ not strict enough...

We didn' t let them out to play enough/ shouldn't let them out in the heat...

They did too much writing / too many activities... We just couldn´t win ...

But if all that was difficult it wasn't quite as scary as the day one of the teachers decided to do glass painting with the students in the afternoon, which was taken up with more "fun" activities as the heat was building- the mornings reserved for more formal classes.

One of the students named James was nine years old.

He was a nice lad but had some health problems and learning difficulties and behavioural problems as a result.

His mother had warned us but in fact he had fitted in well and was one of our favourites as he was in fact very endearing and sweet.

All the students especially liked the Spanish teacher Carolina, she just had such a lovely way with kids.

That fateful day she had decided to do some glass painting with the children, they had all brought in a glass jar or bottle and she was showing them how to blow paint from a straw to make patterns.

When I look back on it know I can see it was a recipe for disaster, but I plead innocence as in fact I was in another classroom teaching adults and didn´t actually know what was happening until the receptionist burst in to my classroom in a panic to ask what she should do.

Apparently, James had sucked the paint in instead of blowing it out and had immediately started to convulse, his eyes rolling back in his head.

That is how I found him on the sofa in reception.

Twitching, foaming at the mouth, his very slender little body convulsing, his heatbeat terrifyingly erratic and only the whites of his eyes to be seen..

A very scary scenario, we needed to get medical help and soon ...

To be continued...

CHAPTER 23- NIGHTMARE SUMMER SCHOOL/ PESADILLA DE ESCUELA DE VERANO PART II

Absolute panic ensued but we quickly established that the paint was non-toxic so we had no idea why this might have happened.

I rang 112, the equivalent of 999, and requested an ambulance immediately.

I have often said, and I truly believe, that the Spanish Health system is fantastic and feel lucky to be living here with the marvellous facilities we have.

However, I have learned that it is not a good idea to get ill in July and August, as the huge influx of tourists stretches these facilities to breaking point. I was told that there were no ambulances immediately available, but when I explained the situation, they said they would try their best.

We tried without success to contact James's mother, who had her phone switched off. James was still fitting and unconscious on the sofa, and I was really convinced that he would die before the ambulance got there.

Finally, after what seemed hours but was probably about 20 minutes, a guy came rushing in and said he was there to take James to hospital.

There were several issues with this.

-One, the guy was only a driver, not a paramedic, and in fact was not trained in any way.

He had just been called in to help in the busy holiday period.

-Two, he was alone, so we had to get James down the stairs on a stretcher between us.

-Three, the fantastic local hospital we have now had not yet been built and the nearest hospital was in fact at least thirty minutes away.

When I saw the antiquated ambulance that awaited us, I realised it would probably take more like 45 minutes.

As he had no helper with him and we had not been able to contact James' mum, I had to accompany James, so he was not alone in the back.

We got him down the stairs on a stretcher and onto the back, and I climbed in also. We set off. It was hot and stifling as there was no air con in the very old ambulance and James was still twitching.

He was unconscious and very pale.

As we drove to the hospital, we seemed to go over every bump in the road.

Suddenly, about half way there, James had a very violent convulsion, his eyes rolled back in his head, then suddenly he went limp and it did not look as if he was breathing.

I panicked and told the driver this, he drove faster and finally we arrived at the hospital.

I was so relieved that we would finally see a doctor, and also to see James was in fact breathing although still unconscious.

I got out of the ambulance, and they rushed to the door to take James out on the stretcher.

As they did so, in their haste they jolted it against the side of the door and James´s eyes opened.

He looked bewildered and dazed, wondering where he was but he was not convulsing any more.

15 minutes later he was sat up in bed on a ward as if nothing had happened and the doctor was testily asking me why I had called an ambulance when he was obviously fine.

Another 15 minutes later and the mother arrived, also seemingly a bit annoyed that she had been dragged away from whatever she was doing when he was sat up in bed chatting away and seemed perfectly ok.

James himself could remember exactly nothing of the whole experience and so could not back me up.

He was given the usual tests but nothing was amiss, so he was discharged almost immediately and everyone seemed to blame me for this waste of their time.

Needless to say, there was no more glass painting in the class.

The following summer I reduced the hours at the summer school and increased the price and as a result the students that came were much more serious about learning Spanish and the parents much less inclined to treat it as a merely a dumping ground for their children.

That summer passed uneventfully thank goodness...

CHAPTER 24- VIAJE DE DISASTRE AL PALACIO DE BENIDORM/ DISASTROUS TRIP TO BENIDORM PALACE

Many of my students were asking me about what there was to do around the area, and for some unknown reason I decided to organise a trip to Benidorm Palace, which is a great venue for a show and a nice meal.

Benidorm is only an hour and a bit away and I organised a coach to take us.

Almost 90 people signed up to come along.

In those days I was still perhaps naive in relying on organisational skills of other companies in Spain.

I booked Benidorm Palace for us, we were scheduled to leave at 18:00 and arrive in plenty of time for the meal which began at 21:00.

Everyone arrived outside the academy on time and all we needed was for the bus to arrive so we could be on our way...

10 minutes passed...

Another 10...

No sign of the bus ...

There was no internet those days, no Whatsapp and Facebook, so I had to go into the building and start looking for numbers to ring to try and find out what had happened to the bus.

Finally, I got through to the office and they contacted the driver to see where he was.

It transpired he was in a double decker bus.

This bus would not fit under the arch that you had to pass through to come down to the academy, so he was waiting at the end of this road and had been for 30 minutes.

For some unexplained reason he must have thought that we would all know this by osmosis and hadn't felt the need to actually ring either me or the office to let us know.

So off we all plodded to the end of the road to find the bus waiting for us out of sight.

When I say the driver was surly and uncooperative I am painting a nice picture.

He was a miserable, awkward xx??? and he proceeded to do anything he could to make the journey as slow and difficult as possible.

He had a “lady” companion with him on the bus which I found later was strictly not allowed and was most likely his mistress.

Anyone who has travelled on a bus in this part of Spain will know that it is an experience not to be forgotten.

I have been present on a coach filled with disabled children where the driver got drunk in the lunch break…

I have travelled by bus from my little village into town when the driver was talking non-stop on his mobile….

And after a run in with a bus driver who seemed to think my car was badly parked outside my own house I was asked by the Policia Local just to humour him, as everyone knew how difficult and awkward bus drivers were…

However, I didn’t know all this then, I was just thinking-

Ah well we still had plenty of time and at least we were on our way....

The next problem occurred when I realised he wasn't going to go on the motorway, he was taking the Coast Road which would take at least 30 minutes longer.

I challenged him on this and he said he wasn't allowed to take the motorway right from the start as the Bus Company wouldn't pay the multiple Toll fees, only the main one that couldn't be avoided.

Great...

The journey continued, we all started to relax a bit as we were well and truly on our way and should arrive within an hour and a half

When we finally got on to the motorway I really relaxed as within 40 minutes we should have arrived.

That was when disaster struck- smoke started to come out of the engine and Mr Belligerent pulled over on to the hard shoulder.

Many gesticulations and head scratching followed, and I was presented with the news that we would have to wait for 2 new buses to arrive as this one needed towing away!!

All the 90 people got off the bus and waited behind the safety barrier trying to make the best of a bad situation.

I clearly remember hearing one nice person comment-

"-She couldn´t organise a piss up in a brewery", and I just remember thinking why the hell had I not organised one of them instead?

I was absolutely dying for a drink by then and I'm still not quite sure how they figured that a bus breaking down was my fault but hey ho....

I called the Benidorm Palace to tell them we would be arriving late, and they said that as there was so many of us they would put the whole thing on hold until we arrived!!

I think we constituted around 80% of their audience that night...

FINALLY, the new buses arrived, two single deckers instead of the one double decker and we all got on. Surely now we would arrive without further incident?

No of course not, everything comes in threes as I realised when suddenly I saw that we were passing the skyscrapers of Benidorm on the right-hand side, the driver had missed the turn off and the bus behind had followed him.

We had to come off at the next exit which I think was Calpe and come back to Benidorm along the Coast Road, another half an hour lost.

We finally reached our destination at around 22.30 and as we entered we were greeted by a huge round of applause. The audience that was already there was ecstatic that at last their evening could start too.

I think the rest of the evening went well enough, nice meal and good entertainment as is the norm at Benidorm Palace.

To be honest for me it was all a blur, and I was so stressed I could not relax and enjoy it.

At the end of the night I was dismayed to see that the original bus driver had returned to take us home, Mr Belligerent, and I had to be talked into getting on the bus again by his lady friend.

This time the journey went without incident, and we finally arrived home in the early hours of the morning, exhausted and relieved to be home safely.

The following week I went to the bus company and put in a formal complaint.

It transpired that Mr Belligerent should have been able to repair the problem on the motorway easily, it was a small thing. They simply did not understand why he had called for replacement buses.

I gathered his lady friend may have been the reason for this, this way he had an evening with just the two of them. However, he was in fact not allowed to take unauthorised people on his bus so she should not have been there in the first place.

He was suspended for 3 months- apparently, they wanted to sack him, but he was on a permanent contract and therefore they could not- and as compensation I was offered free transport to a place of my choosing for me and anyone else who was brave enough to go on another trip...

This time I choose meal and Flamenco dancing in Torrevieja, much closer to home. We had a great time, but it was the last trip I organised.

I just could not face it again.

CHAPTER 25- DOG LOVER DANGER/ PELIGRO PARA AMANTES DE PERROS

Recently I have been reminded of another interpreter rather than teacher experience I had many years ago around this time of year.

One Saturday I received a frantic phone call from a lady called Rene. I had done the NIE numbers and residencias for her and her husband, Ian, and they were now settled down and enjoying their new life.

On this particular day however, she was extremely worried about Ian's health.

-"I am outside your house" she said.

-"I have Ian in the car he has been ill for a week. At first we thought it was the flu. He has a temperature, he is woozy and can hardly stand, and he can´t keep anything down. His joints are aching, and he is incoherent. It is not getting better though and I am really worried about him. Can you come with us to the hospital please?"

I couldn´t refuse she was so panicky, and off we went.

I could see Ian was quite delirious, so I agreed that she had done the right thing, he needed to see a doctor.

On arrival they tested his blood pressure, heart and took some blood tests. The blood tests would take several hours for the results to come back and in the meantime the very helpful lady doctor was mystified as all his vital signs were fine, but he was clearly quite poorly.

There was no flu around at that time as it was summer.

As she continued examining him the cleaner entered and started to clean the floors. Spanish hospitals are generally spotlessly clean and always scrubbed often.

-"Can you think of anything different at all apart from the general feeling of being unwell that you have noticed lately?" asked the doctor, puzzled

-"No, nothing" Ian replied, then suddenly he said:

"Actually, I have got a spot on the top of my leg that has been there about a week, it seems to be getting bigger. "

I reported this back to the doctor and Ian took off his trousers so she could have a look.

Ian had quite hairy legs and up at the top of his left leg buried in the hair was an angry red spot, quite raised and easily visible.

As we looked at it the cleaner came over to look too and pronounced -"Parece una garrapata", or in other words "It looks like a tick"...

The doctor produced a pair of tweezers and removed the revolting insect. It had attached to the hair on Ian's leg as he was walking his dog in the campo wearing shorts, then it had burrowed in and was making him ill.

Removal of the creature and a course of antibiotics was the cure, along with the advice not to wear shorts in the campo if you have hairy legs!!

On the way home, Ian, a retired detective inspector from Manchester commented:

"It was the cleaner what sussed it"

Classic....

CHAPTER 26- Fxx??ING FLIP FLOPS/ CHANCLAS MALDITAS (POLITE VERSION!)

These days I have few children's classes, my students are mainly adults. I do like teaching children in general but it depends on the child.

More often than not, it in fact depends on the parents. Most young children will pick up Spanish once they have done a few months at mainstream school, provided that they have been prepared a bit at least with some basic school vocabulary and are encouraged by their parents.

It is much more difficult for older children as their own language is more firmly ensconced and the desire to learn has to come from them.

In my experience there is nothing on this earth that will make a teenager sit down and learn something they have no interest in.

With younger children you can always find something that they do like such as football or animals and use that as a tool.

Teenagers however are quite specific in their interests which normally only revolve around their peers so are much more difficult.

Having said that, a teenager who is actually interested in Spanish is the best student you can have, their ability and aptitude are stunning. If they are not, classes are a painful experience for both student and teacher :(

Once a lady came along to me for classes for her 2 sons aged 7 and 12. She insisted on sitting in the classes despite me telling her what a bad idea that was.

As we all know, children tend to behave worse in front of their parents and these two were no exception. The class was an hour long and they would not sit and concentrate, they ran around the classroom and tipped chairs over and quite frankly this lady was throwing her money away.

I tried to tell her so, but she still insisted on coming to class.

In the third torturous class the 7-year-old insisted on removing his flip flop and banging it on the table.

Normally I would be the one to try and keep the class in order but as the mother was there that makes it difficult for me, so I sat back and waited. Surely now she would tell him off.

I looked at her expectantly as little Johnny continued to bang the flip flop on the table on top of the work he should have been doing. It seemed to go on forever but at last she grabbed him and screamed in his face:

"Put the fucking flip flop down and get on with your work".

Not quite the discipline that I was expecting...

CHAPTER 27- BEWARE OF BOGUS INTERPRETERS/ CUIDADO CON LOS INTÉRPRETES FALSOS

A conversation that came up in class the other day reminded me of how easy it is to be taken in by bogus interpreters. If you don´t know much Spanish someone just saying "café con leche" can sound fluent. I have listened to some absolute scammers in my years of interpreting in various situations.

One such incident I remember was at the Guardia Civil.

I was there with a client to make a "denuncia" (police statement) after a house break-in.

There was one person waiting before we arrived, an elderly man with his male "interpreter".

I heard the interpreter turn to his client and say:

-"Ok just leave it to me".

He proceeded to attempt to explain to the Guardia at the desk what they were there for in the worst Spanish imaginable.

Effectively putting the "o" on the end of everything as the stereotypical Brit. The Guardia, agent of an organisation not renowned for helpfulness at the best of times, stared at him blankly and pointed to the sign displayed at the side of the window that said in Spanish that they would not attend to anyone without an interpreter.

-"No te entiendo, tienes que volver con traductor" he said.

(I don´t understand you, you have to return with a translator)

The "translator" turned to his client and said:-

"They are too busy to take a statement today we have to come back another time"

Shocking!

Another time I was in the queue with clients requiring an NIE number (Número de Identidad de Extranjero- Foreigner's Identification Number)

In front of us was an representative of an Estate Agent that I knew quite well with his clients who needed the number to buy a house.

-"What does NIE stand for?" -They asked

-"National Insurance España" -Was the immediate reply.

Really??????

Some people never want to admit they just do not know something, so they make it up instead.

Or maybe once someone had told him that, and he kept telling other people. They would tell other people, who would tell other people- and ad infinitum.

Then there you are with hundreds of Brits with the wrong information.

CHAPTER 28- YOU JUST GET BY DON´T YOU---- DO YOU?

Vera and Doug were one of those couples that did everything at a hundred miles an hour, even though they were retired and had been in Spain for quite some time. None of the Spanish laid back attitude had rubbed off on them whatsoever.

They came to me for interpreter service as Vera was in desperate need of a hip replacement. They told me how she had been on the top of the urgent waiting list for over a year now, but she was in so much pain they wanted to take me along to see if the process could be sped up a bit.

They had never used an interpreter before, they thought it was a waste of money.

When I asked where they had learnt Spanish they replied:

-"Oh, we don´t speak Spanish".

So I asked how then did they knew all this information, that she was on the top of the list etc?

They had used phrases such as "they said this" and "they told us that"

"Oh, you just get by don´t you, you get the gist"

Do you?

Anyway, we barely made it to the hospital with our lives as Doug was driving so fast in the sun and had failed to see that a car in front had stopped and was indicating to turn left.

There is nothing worse than a backseat driver so I didn´t say anything hoping he had noticed.

When it became obvious he in fact hadn´t, I screamed "stop" and he screeched to a halt just in time.

At the hospital, it transpired that in fact they had no record of Vera whatsoever and she was not even on the list at all never mind the top of it,

After "wasting their money" on an interpreter Vera got her new hip within 3 months.

Maybe they hadn´t quite got "the gist" of it after all.

CHAPTER 29- FINDING KENNY/ BUSCANDO A KENNY

Some of you who have attended classes in the past will know that a couple of years ago I was lucky enough to find someone to help out with everything, Sarah.

Sarah was a lovely young girl, a previous student and as with many of my students we became friends.

Sarah and her boyfriend Scott had been looking for a dog. Not just any dog, the perfect dog for them. As you all know, there are many dogs looking for homes. A little overwhelmed, eventually Sarah declared she was going to stop looking and that the right dog would find her...

One of the many helpful things Sarah did was to take my little dog Rocky for a walk. One particular morning she took him out at a different time than normal as she wasn´t feeling well and was going to finish early...

Fate..

Especially as I had in fact sent her a message to say not to worry, I would take him after class, but she didn't receive it in time and off they went.

10 minutes later she sent me a message with a photo of a dog asking if I recognised him as he was following her and Rocky.

Male, castrated, small, reasonably well looked after but no collar.

I didn’t recognise the dog, but said to her to bring him back here.

She did.

He came with her happily.

He had a drink and something to eat and it was clear he was quite a young dog with a lovely temperament.

I said we should take him to the local vets to see if he had a chip as it was clear he had at some point belonged to someone. Sarah proclaimed then and there that if he didn´t have a chip she wanted to keep him and she would call him "Kenny" as this was the name her and her boyfriend had already decided on for when for they found the right dog.

So at lunch time off we went to the local vet. As soon as he passed the machine over the little dog the ensuing "beep" told us that he had indeed already been chipped which meant he had an owner and Sarah´s face fell. The vet duly called the owner and an amazing story unravelled.

This little boy had been rescued by a Spanish girl (the current owner) from the "perrera" (dog pound) when only a tiny puppy and was living with the girl´s father in a "casa de campo" (country house) with 2 other dogs.

Unfortunately, subsequently her father had died and the dogs were now living there alone with an employee feeding them every day.

The girl and her partner lived miles away and couldn´t have the dogs with them but tried to visit for the weekend every couple of weeks.

Little "Kenny" had escaped once before by digging under the fence and later returned, but this time he had been gone **3 MONTHS** and the country house was 30 kilometres away from where Sarah had found him.

Another mystery was that the previous owner could see that he had at some point been clipped as his hair was shorter- so somewhere in this meantime he had been with people. But they had not checked if he had a microchip!!!

The girl loved him but could not be with him all the time so she realised he would be better with Sarah in a home always with people than back at the "casa del campo" just with the dogs. He would probably only escape again. She agreed to sign him over. Sarah was so happy her "Kenny" had found her.

We asked the Spanish girl what his name was......and she answered:

"Ken"

You could not make it up........

CHAPTER 30- ECCENTRIC DONALD- DONALD EL TIO RARO

Donald was a typical "eccentric" British guy. Tall, bald with big ears and the look of a more handsome and not green Shrek, I knew he was a little eccentric from the day he came to have a look around. It was Christmas, and always at Christmastime I give my students Spanish liquors and turrón or some other nice Spanish traditional treat.

Turrón or polverones are the Spanish equivalent of Quality Street, Roses or Matchmakers at Christmas.

Donald appeared as if by magic at coffee time to discuss classes. I gave him some Ponche (Spanish brandy liquor) to try and a coffee and chocolate as he chatted and watched the class.

30 minutes later he was still there showing no signs of moving.

Another 30 minutes passed... and another---

I was starting to think he would never go home.

Anyway "no pasa nada" as he eventually signed up and along he came for the next course.

A few things he did during the course proved his eccentricity—

Disappearing to the loo with a packet of baby wipes,

Wearing earplugs in class.

Telling many interesting stories that led to me referring to him as an international man of mystery, 003 and a half.

But I will always remember Donald most fondly as the student who gave me the best excuse ever for not attending class-

He emailed me one day to say he would not be in the following day as his living room window had been shot by a gun.

He had to wait in for the glaziers to fit bullet proof glass throughout all his house.

To prove this had really happened he sent me a photo of the bullet hole.

To this day no one has come up with a better excuse :)

CHAPTER 31- NOT THE OTHER WOMAN THIS TIME/ NO SOY LA OTRA ESTA VEZ

In my life I have done things, as I imagine has everyone, that I have regretted.

Søren Kierkegaard said that life can only be understood backwards, but that it must be lived forwards. So on we go, doing the best we can, but often totally messing up by doing things which seemed like a good idea at the time. Sometimes hurting other people.

I have been guilty of this many times, and a victim of it too.

However, I believe in karma and accepting responsibility, so I try to forgive and move on from those who have hurt me and accept readily the karma I deserve for those that I have hurt.

It really annoys me though, to be wrongly accused without even having enjoyed the pleasure of whatever naughty thin I am accused of!!

This happened to me once with a student. I will call him Jacob.

Jacob came for classes for quite a while with no incident. I knew he had a long-term partner and to be honest nothing untoward happened or was said for many months. Then one weekend, out of the blue, I received a private message from him.

It would be rude not to reply to a student, so I did. It was something banal, I don´t really remember now what the original message was. This started a flurry of messages over the next few weeks which gradually (on his part I might add) became more and more risque.

´This was quite tricky for me as I was torn between the fact I had not long split up from someone so was quite enjoying the attention. Also, that he was a student so I did not really want to upset him, and also I found him vaguely attractive in an inexplicable way. :)

I reminded him- "Don`t you have a live-in girlfriend?"

" It´s complicated" came the predictable reply.

However, I was very well behaved and none of my messages could have been construed as anything more than friendship and possibly at the very worst a mild flirting.

This went on for a couple of weeks until one evening we were in the middle of a messenger conversation, and he abruptly disappeared.

This was unusual for him to go without a farewell, so I suppose I knew that something was wrong. The next day he was due in for class, and then early in the morning I realised I had a message from a woman I did not know. Guess who? Yes Jacob´s live in partner.

Well, it was obvious from the message she thought that something was going on between us. I was told in no uncertain terms that I should be ashamed of myself for breaching the "teacher/student" barrier (for God´s sake he was more 50 than 15). Also was I aware that he had cheated on her with at least two of her friends, one of which was staying at their house so in their own home?

Well, no I was not aware of that but then he was not my partner so why should I be? And if she was aware of it why was she even still with him?

I put these questions to her in the most diplomatic way I could, and to be fair she did apologise. Apparently, she had caught him messaging me the evening before and jumped to the wrong conclusion, presumably based on his previous form.

After a brief conversation she even referred to me as an "angel".

Nope most definitely not one of those but in this particular case innocent of all charges...

She then proceeded to share her thoughts and experiences with him publicly on Facebook, so I was very happy that I had resisted that temptation and I felt very lucky not to have been dragged anymore into it.

It then transpired that besides the previous affairs and trying to start something with me, he was also already having an affair with another woman!!

So I was more of a smokescreen for her I think.

I did tell him what I thought of him, and perhaps predictably he did not come for any more Spanish Classes. Which is a shame because I did quite like him really.

So anyway, that was one time I did get hung for a sheep when I was for once, really a lamb.

CHAPTER 32-MELANIE THE TROLL / MELANIE LA TROLL

For once with this person, I am using their real name. If in fact it is their real name as I know of several used by her.

I don´t feel the need to protect her identity as she is in fact a very nasty person as you will see.

The Internet age has brought many positive benefits to my little school. Previously newspaper advertising was the only way to get your name out there in the area and was quite expensive. Interested students would contact by telephone only, which is a rarity these days.

In fact if the phone rings now we all look at each other like- what the hell is that?

These days Facebook is my most effective advertising medium, and enquiries come in the most part through messenger, email or even WhatsApp- very few telephone calls.

I also, thanks to Internet searches for Spanish classes, receive enquiries from many different nationalities. I can advertise my books for sale all over Spain and even the world, along with my YouTube Channel. These are the positives.

The negative is that once you put yourself out there into the public spectrum you have to accept that not everyone thinks you are great :).

People make comments. 99 % of the time the comments are positive, but you always remember the 1% that are not more unfortunately.

I have come to realise that famous people must need to be very mentally strong or, more likely, have someone else to deal with their social media if my modest little experience with internet exposure is anything to go by. I have learnt that some people are just plain nasty, and I have also learnt hide, remove block are the best ways of dealing with them- engagement is not advisable.

Melanie is something else. In Melanie I found my first real "troll"- someone who really seemed to have a personal grudge against me that made a concerted effort over time to make my life difficult. Why? I have no idea, but this is the story.

Melanie contacted me regarding classes by email, saying she had done some Spanish before and was interested in an intensive course. As she was a

"Celta qualified teacher"(take note of this- it will come up again :)) she felt she could progress quite quickly.

I explained to her how the classes worked, i.e. small groups students working individually within the group, and eventually her husband emailed to book her in. Maybe I should have known something when he at first was reluctant to do so, saying he didn`t want to be "scammed".

In my experience trolls use a lot of this emotive language- "scam" "scum" "lowlife" etc, and it did seem a bit of a strange thing to say. He then sent me all his credit card details by email as he seemed to have problems using the online payment facility and asked me to do it!

Lucky for him I am not "scum" and I don´t "scam"

So along came Melanie on her first day and seemed pleasant enough. She signed her enrolment form and settled into the class. The only real problems that first day were that her phone rang and pinged incessantly, and she did not know how to silence it, but in the end another student did it for her.

Also, every 15 minutes she was going outside to smoke a cigarette, and as she was doing the same work as 2 of the other students we had to wait for her, but it was ok because she was a "Celta trained teacher" so she could easily catch up...

Another problem was that at 12.00 she started packing up, although the class actually is until 13.00. She seemed surprised though I don´t know why as the timetable was clearly given to her on several emails. Anyway, in general the first morning passed well enough and she seemed happy and looking forward to the next class. Her husband (also a Celta trained teacher apparently □) came to pick her up and that was it for day one.

Day 2 did not go so well. Her fag breaks got longer and I couldn´t keep the other students of her level waiting as they did not smoke and were progressing well through the work.

So after about her 4th break in an hour I gently suggested that I move on with the other 2 and she carry on at her own pace, as also the others seem to be picking up things more quickly, I just didn´t want her to feel under pressure to finish quickly and it was not fair to make them wait.

Oh dear. She proceeded to tell me my method was rubbish, and as a "Celta Trained teacher" she knew you should not have different levels in the same class.

Before I knew it, she had packed up her stuff and left to have another cigarette outside while her Celta trained husband came to pick her up.

The class was so much nicer after she left.

That evening I received an email asking for her money back. I pointed out to her that on both the website and the enrolment form she had signed it states clearly that money is not refundable. She could convert to private classes or an E course if she liked?

I began to realise that Melanie liked a drink before writing these emails as they grew gradually more ridiculous. I did look for her on Facebook then with the intention of blocking as I had a feeling she would be trouble.

I could not find her on there, I now realise why as not only she was using a slightly different name her profile picture must have been at least 30 years old, photo shopped, or not her at all.

The next news from Melanie was that she asked to come and sign the complaints book, as in Spain anyone has the right to do who is not happy with a product or service. Along she duly came with her husband, two Celta trained teachers together, and she completed it in English (!) and took off the copy.

I knew they had absolutely no idea what to do with it then and obviously I wasn´t going to help them on that.

A couple of weeks later I received an email from PayPal, through whom I manage my online payment facility.

They had opened a dispute and frozen Mr Carey´s payment as he had sent them a written complaint that went something like this:

- " I paid for the course in advance and when I got there on the day it was due to start, there was no course. I feel I have been scammed"

Liar.

This is where I did make a mistake. I tried to deal with this dispute by email, sending the enrolment form and attendance sheet to Paypal to prove the course had started, and also stating that the other students on the course had offered to provide evidence that Melanie had started the course and what had happened.

I have learnt from this that PayPal email section just wants the proof of postage of an item, if it is a service you need to speak to a person. I think it must be an electronic service by email and it doesn´t look into specific more complicated cases.

The dispute was found in his favour and I was furious that his money was returned to him.

However, I then called PayPal and spoke directly to an agent. It took a little while to get through but when I did the agent was extremely understanding and I could explain the whole situation. She was very apologetic and within 10 minutes the money was back in my account. Unfortunately, it was too late to take it back from him so in fact it was PayPal who had lost out. Imagine that, two "Celta trained" teachers had scammed PayPal!!

I also found out that Melanie had been on Amazon and rated my books (even though she has never used them or bought them) with one star and the comment "dreadful".

Such a lovely woman. Probably something to do on another drunken evening in her sad life.

The whole experience was upsetting and awful but time passed and I just chalked it down to experience. That had never happened to me before and I hope will never happen to me again.

That someone would actually search out ways of getting to me like the Amazon thing was just awful.

I know you can´t please all the people all the time so I just presumed that was the end of it.

A whole year passed, and she faded into distant memory. Then one Sunday morning I started to receive messages from several people I knew telling me to look on a local "shaming" Facebook site.

I joined the group to investigate but the post had been removed. Luckily one of my friends had sent me a screen shot. It was a post from someone called Melanie Jane and went something like this:

"Be careful of Vicky Riley (spelt my name wrong) Spanish teacher in San Miguel de Salinas. As a Celta trained teacher myself, I found her teaching methods very strange. After a bit of nastiness, I received a full refund". Grrrrr

I posted an answer, tagging her. I explained exactly what had happened and questioned, "who in fact is the scammer?" As I say, no wonder I hadn´t been able to find her on Facebook as not only the name was different (I had known her as Melanie Torres, and Melanie Carey, but the photo was so different from what she actually looks like, a mid to late 50´s woman, that it was either photo shopped or in fact a photo of her daughter or someone else entirely.

I was heartened by the messages of support I received.

Melanie had not endeared herself to the other members of the site with a previous comment that "this area is full of scammers from the North of England". Ha ha bit of a sweeping statement Melanie?

How to make friends and influence people lol.

Well later that day she obviously recovered from that morning's hangover- I am convinced that her nasty posts are result of too much alcohol.

I am now blocked and have blocked her in return. Maybe in some parallel Facebook universe she is still saying nasty things about me, who knows? I just think it is a strange way for a Celta trained teacher to behave...

Melanie Jane, Torres, Carey or whatever your name is- if you are reading this (firstly actually why?- still trolling?) remember that Karma is a bitch. I feel sorry for anyone that can hold a grudge for so long despite the fact they scammed their money back and can always be happy in the fact they are a CELTA TRAINED teacher.

CHAPTER 33- CURTAINGATE/ LA HISTORIA DE LAS CORTINAS

In the Ex-Pat community, we have a special qualification that we call the "Gatwick Diploma".

People get on the plane at Gatwick (or any other airport as one thing and miraculously on the way over to Spain some metamorphosis happens, and they get off the plane as something completely different.

For example, someone who has never built anything in their lives suddenly becomes a master builder offering building services, or someone who has only ever made beans on toast becomes a professional chef.

Part of this is due to the fact it is so difficult to find work in Spain, so often you have to turn your hand to just about anything to survive financially.

It is also due to the fact that many people are total blaggers who completely re-invent themselves, secure in the knowledge no one checks up on anything.

Some people are serious con artists who rip vulnerable people off for a lot of money, and others do it on a smaller scale.

Mike the handyman was one of these.

My classroom has a staircase at the side up which in the winter heat escapes. One year I had the brilliant idea of getting curtains put up which would prevent this happening and make the classroom warmer. I debated about doing it myself and decided as it is quite a long pole needed it would be better to have someone professional do it. I advertised on local Facebook sites and Mike sent me a message sounding very professional and I asked him to come along and give me a quote.

Along he came, measured up, seemed to know exactly what he was doing.

However, the quote he came back with was for 180 euros including the curtains. I had budgeted 120 euros, thinking really this is not a complicated job for someone who knows what they are doing.

He quite sniffily insisted the curtains were top quality, lined, and would fit exactly so no alterations necessary.

That´s why the price was as it was. I hummed and hawed thinking it seemed expensive, but I know you do get what you pay for a lot of the time, so maybe it was worth it just to get it done properly.

How wrong I was. Even after all these years living in Spain sometimes it feels that I haven´t learnt anything.

Mike turned up one lunchtime.

I felt an hour would easily be long enough as he had already measured up so he would be gone before the next class turned up.

After 30 minutes of measuring and cutting poles without any results I realised things were maybe not going to plan.

There was a lot of pulling of the poles one way and then the other as if this would miraculously make them fit better. The curtains came out of the pack, went up, came down, went up came down. More pacing and measuring ensued,

An hour passed. My students arrived. We were all fascinated.

Suddenly he pronounced he was finished and started packing up. The curtains were stretched to fit the poles and as he had put the said poles up unevenly, they were far too long on one side.

Also, they had been put up strangely in a vain attempt to make them fit better. I made him adjust them one more time which he did with bad grace, reluctantly paid him and off he went 180 euros better off for a terrible job.

I had to take up the curtains as they were far too long and add two more to make a proper fit. So much for not having to make any alterations.

Needless to say, I never used Mike´s services again.

However, I see on Facebook he is still around and people often recommend him.

Maybe that is his friends or family...

Maybe I just got him on a bad day---

Or maybe curtain pole putting up is just not his thing....

Así es la vida :)

CHAPTER 34-WHAT HAPPENED TO UNCLE JIMMY?/ QUE PASÓ A TIO JAIME?

Anyone who has lived in Spain and had to deal with bureaucracy in any way shape or form will get this next story.

If you haven´t, you may think it is exaggerated or couldn´t possibly be true.

In Spain, we have to get used to what I call "the run-around".

Basically, this is where you are told one thing by one person, and something else by another.

Rules are completely arbitrary, and decisions are often made depending on a following wind and if there is an "r" in the month.

Even official ones.

If you are a person who likes organisation, order and to know exactly where you are, Spain is simply not the country for you. There is no communication between official departments, you basically have to throw yourself on their mercy, do all the legwork yourself, hope for the best, and if you are lucky, you will get sorted.

Never make the cardinal mistake of getting angry or irritated, the shutter will come down and you will completely be blanked. Patience is everything if you want co-operation and help from anyone who has a bit of power in their role.

There is generally no point in asking to speak to anyone else either as they are often the only person there who can help, so you have to keep them on your side as much as you can.

Quite a few years ago a friend of mine asked me to go to help her communicate at Torrevieja hospital.

Her and her dad were worried about her "uncle" Jimmy.

He wasn´t her real uncle, he was a good life-long friend of her dad, who was working away at the time and had asked her to try and find out what had happened to him.

Jimmy had disappeared.

Nearly a week earlier, Jimmy had become ill in the middle of the night at his home where he lived alone. Neighbours reported that they had called an ambulance which had spirited him away and he hadn´t been seen since.

Presumably he had been taken to the hospital but he hadn´t contacted anyone since and he had left his mobile in the house so no one could call him either.

Jimmy was a guy in his very late sixties who had a touch of dementia or Alzheimers and didn´t speak any Spanish. He had no other family, and they were concerned he wouldn´t have been able to communicate at the hospital.

Also, the worst might have even happened as he had a bad heart, and he could be lying in the morgue with no one to claim his body!!

So that evening off we went to Torrevieja hospital.

In my experience you rarely get anyone on receptions, customer help desks etc that actually want to help. Customer service is so badly named.

Unfortunately for us, the girl on reception that evening (Cristina- I will never forget her name), was one of the unhelpful types...

I explained the situation to her, that Uncle Jimmy was very vulnerable due to his mental and physical state, and we were trying to find him. I told her when he was probably admitted and that he may not have even been able to communicate his name.

She said that she had no record of anyone admitted of that name so I asked, had anyone been admitted that evening that they had listed as "desconocido" or unknown?

He may even have died as it was a suspected heart attack he was taken away with.

Well, wouldn´t you think that they would want to find out the identity of any unknown patient or corpse they had?

Nooooo. Cristina refused to even look in the records and said we would have to get permission from the Guardia Civil (police) before she could give out any information.

I was still calm at this point and asked if maybe she could ring the Guardia and ask their permission to give us the information.

No, she couldn´t do that. We had to go to the police station ourselves and come back with a written permission.

I feel I should point out at this point for those who don´t know that Torrevieja hospital is small. It is not like a big City hospital where maybe there would be several "desconocidos" who had been brought in.

Anyway in Spain you are supposed to carry ID at all times, so it would have been unusual for someone to be brought in without it. How many elderly foreign people with no family or Id would have been brought in that night anyway? One- Uncle Jimmy!! But she refused to help.

Off we went.

The Guardia we were assigned was very helpful, or at least pleasant. He predictably told us that what Cristina had told us was rubbish. We did not need written permission, she could tell us if anyone "unknown" was in the hospital, either dead or alive as obviously they would want to solve the mystery of who they were. He would not give us anything in writing or come back with us to the hospital.

However, he did kindly ring the hospital and he definitely spoke to someone!

I heard the conversation with my own ears, it was a woman he was speaking to.

He explained the situation and said there was no reason we shouldn´t be given any information necessary to find out what had happened to hapless uncle Jimmy, who we were getting more and more worried about with every passing hour.

He came off the phone and told us it was all sorted, we should go back to the hospital and they would look in the computer to see who had been brought in that night and if there were any "desconocidos" amongst them.

Reassured, we went back to the hospital to speak once more with the (not so) lovely Cristina.

We walked in hopefully, but our hopes were soon dashed when I told her of our experience with the Guardia.

She completely denied any knowledge of this phone call from him!!

She all but accused us of lying, and said the situation was the same. No written permission no information.

I have to admit I was starting to get a little bit miffed by now (understatement).

Two wasted hours and nothing achieved.

I could see in the booth behind her there were several telephonists, all female, so my guess is the Guardia had spoken to one of them not Cristina.

I asked her politely would she mind asking them if they had taken the call if it wasn´t her?

He had definitely spoken to someone as I had heard the conversation myself.

She refused.

I know I had to get away from her as I would say something I regretted.

As I mentioned, Torrevieja is a small hospital.

I took my friend´s arm and said to the delightful Cristina we were going to find him ourselves. If she refused to simply check the admissions for the night that he was whisked away on the computer we would check every room one by one.

Off we went. 15 minutes later we found Uncle Jimmy on the first-floor tucking into his evening meal and seemingly none the worse for his experience.

He was labelled "desconocido", and he seemed to be quite happy in there, nice and warm in a private room being fed three times a day and looked after.

I left them together to get sorted and returned to my new best friend Cristina for a few choice words just to make me feel better.

She did have the grace to look a little bit abashed, when she realised we had not been making the whole story up. I mean, really? what would have been the point of lying about the whole thing? What advantage could we possibly have gained?

That is really what I will never understand about the whole experience. I totally get the patient confidentiality issue. However, when you have a patient who is obviously confused and can´t tell you who they are, then someone comes along worried about a family member who is confused and was taken off by an ambulance and disappeared on the same night this patient was admitted-?? Why would you treat them with such suspicion?

No lo entiendo!!!!

CHAPTER 35- COVID-19 DIARIES- 1- How it all started

The world has changed forever.

I think what took us all most by surprise was the speed it happened.

It felt like one minute it was just lurking in the background as a particularly Chinese problem, so nothing really for us in Europe to worry about, then it was here affecting all of us and life would never be the same...

For some people, life would end, in a horrible and lonely way.

Others would survive, but after weeks of illness with loved ones having to care for them alone and unsupported due to the infectiousness of it.

Meanwhile, selfish and ignorant people would flout all the rules, not really taking it seriously if they had not been personally affected.

In "el confinemiento" (lockdown) here in Spain, I think we all went a little crazy in the end.

These next couple of blogs will be my experiences.

The first confirmed case of Covid- 19 in Spain was on the 31st January 2020, when a German tourist tested positive in the Canary Islands. By 13th March, cases had been confirmed in all 50 provinces of our country. Concentrated mainly in Madrid, by the 25th of March the death toll had surpassed China (reported cases at least).

On the 2nd of April, 950 people died in Spain of the virus in a 24-hour period—at the time, the most by any country in a single day.

In my area we were sort of aware of what was going on, but we felt it was mainly in Madrid so it didn´t feel real to us I think.

A far- away problem that we didn´t really need to worry about.

I look back now at one particular student telling us her husband was ill and describing his symptoms as:-

"Some sort of chest infection he couldn´t shake off”.

I am now quite certain that it had already arrived here.

Thursday 12th March started like any other day.

Classes began as normal.

Then Lis, my teacher's assistant, casually mentioned that she had gone shopping to the local supermarket the night before and there was NOTHING on the shelves.

Literally nothing.

No pasta, no fresh food, no frozen food, **NADA**.

She told me that many people had arrived at their second homes here on the coast from Madrid to escape the virus, and were stocking up.

That was the start of the madness.

The next day off I went to my supermarket for my normal weekly shop. There was **NOTHING**.

All that was left was one pack of chicken feet which I thought I could probably live without.

Luckily for me, as I have transport, I went to a lesser used supermarket and was able to get what I needed.

The temptation to stockpile is infectious, but the Spanish President Pedro Sanchez had guaranteed the supply of food so I knew we did not have to do this.

Unfortunately other people did not see it in that way.

There are many greedy selfish people out there only thinking of themselves and causing problems for everyone else. Vulnerable people with no transport to get to other places would have been lost.

That Friday, some coastal towns were curfewed by the police as they realised the selfish madrileños had come to their second homes and brought more of the virus with them.

That is my one criticism of the Spanish Government,

Madrid should have been locked down sooner before people could leave to spread it.

By Saturday 14th March, we were all in "confiimiento" as the lockdown began and an "estado de alarma" was declared.

I stupidly chose that very morning to slip in the shower on some hair conditioner and most likely fracture my nose/ cheekbone and maybe break a little bone in my foot. I decided I would not go anywhere near a hospital under the circumstances, and I just hope now they have repaired themselves ok.

By then I had watched a couple of YouTube videos about the virus in China and I was absolutely terrified.

You know when you wish you could unsee something.

So, I developed a nice black eye and decided I would no longer be washing my hair in the shower.

This fall did have a future impact on my health which I will explain in a future blog.

We had all said "goodbye and see you Monday" that Thursday morning, not knowing that in the space of just a couple of days everything was going to change..

CHAPTER 36- COVID DIARIES 2- The 8 o'clock applause

So, there we were in Lockdown (confinamiento), which the Government very cleverly leaked to us bit by bit.

Looking back now, it is inconceivable that we believed it would only by a fortnight, then everything would go back to normal.

It was a shock, but 2 weeks is not very long hey?

I think at first we just decided to get on with it and accepted this was for our own good.

The Spanish Lockdown was very strict, thankfully, and I for one actually hated going out when the virus was at its peak and could not wait to get home, disinfected and safe.

I got on with projects I had been meaning to do, spoke to friends and family much more often than normal, and settled into online classes.

I will be eternally grateful to those students who kept me busy in this way and helped at a time that was not only difficult financially but also mentally.

I will also be eternally grateful to my dogs as at least I was able to get out with them.

However, they did not seem to understand they had to do their business in 15 minutes so it could be a bit stressful sometimes, and very eerie out there to be honest, **NO ONE** out and about.

I always felt that I was in an episode of the Walking Dead.

My white dog Riley in particular is a very private pooper and likes to find a very hidden place normally behind a bush in the campo.

So doing it out in the open on a lead did not go down well with him at all, even if it was cleared up afterwards.

Very soon someone came up with the bright ides of the 8 o'clock applause.

It did start off at 10 o'clock but was soon changed as that is dinner/ supper time here in Spain.

At first it seemed such a lovely idea, applauding and showing appreciation for all the frontline workers who were putting their lives at risk for us.

Not only doctors and nurses, ambulance people, cleaners, supermarket workers bus drivers, refuse collectors, delivery drivers etc. We really found out during this crisis who real essential workers are.

I´m not quite sure why it was decided that it would be every night here, probably to give a structure to people's days and a focus of solidarity.

So it all started off fine, we would all go out clapping whistling etc, banging pots and pans.

This was before the clocks went forward and the weather got warmer.

5 minutes of clapping followed by 10 minutes of neighbours shouting over at each other and that was it. It gave a warm feeling and was often followed by a lap of honour by the Policia Local applauding us all for respecting the Lockdown.

Very civilised.

As time went on it became a torment. The weather got warmer, the clocks went forward so it was still light, and as the weeks went on, I think we all got a bit more stir crazy and paranoid.

I have the misfortune to live in the middle of neighbours who wanted to talk to each other (haven´t they heard of video calls) and they shouted over at each other with my house in the middle.

These conversations got louder and louder and longer and longer, starting at 7:30 and not finishing till 9 o'clock at least.

Sometimes they would just all get together at a gate, no mask, no distancing, sometimes even sharing food off a plate.

Imagine that every night, 7 days a week, I thought I would go crazy.

To cut a long story short, I was definitely made to feel I was the odd one out in not thinking this was acceptable behaviour.

I was even told (not for the first time) to get back to England where I come from (after being here 22 years?).

This neighbour is particularly nasty, after having threatened to kill my cat a few years ago.

Funnily enough, he once was married to and English woman and had children with her.

Maybe this is where the bitterness comes from.

Also, he works in a restaurant in a largely British Commercial Centre so not sure what his customer service is like, or maybe he just doesn´t like me.

That´s fine because I most certainly do not like him.

I have never been so relieved than when this stopped, I had come to absolutely dread it rather than feel like paying respect.

The one silent tribute to the dead announced one Sunday was not respected, in fact I heard my nasty neighbour speak on the phone all the way through it. What a great guy.

Ironically as rules relaxed, they began to do this social gathering less and less, and now the State of Alarm (Estado de Alarma) is over they never do it. ;)

I think we were all having a bit of a meltdown in the midst of it.

I thank God for the "New Normal". (La Nueva Normalidad)

CHAPTER 37- CONSUELO AND COCAINE/ CONSUELO Y LA COCAINA

Yesterday I was helped out in a personal matter by my fellow teacher, Lis, who has worked with me now for over two years and helps out with classes.

I am eternally grateful.

I started to think of all the other teachers I have had working with me over the years, and how fortunate I have been to have so many good helpers. Some have even started as students then become Spanish teachers themselves.

Some work independently now teaching Spanish themselves, in one way my rivals.

I don´t look at it like that, really what better endorsement is there for my teaching method?

I love it

But one teacher I will never forget is Consuelo (not her real name).

I advertised for a teacher, and as usual received many replies. I did not know then, but this is the experience that taught me, that CVs mean very little and neither do qualifications. Teachers are born not made.

Qualifications help, but a week long online Tefl course doth not a teacher make.

Neither does even a teaching degree mean that you can communicate knowledge.

It is an art.

Empathy and intuition is worth twice as much as any qualification or impressive CV.

Well, Consuelo had both... An impressive CV and an impressive teaching degree.

Unfortunately, she was the worst teacher I have ever had, with the possible exception of one British guy at summer school who I will talk about it the next blog.

Certainly, the experience for me was the worst.

She came over well in her interview, a little bossy maybe but that is not a bad thing either for a teacher as you do have to take control sometimes.

She spoke English so she could explain things to the students, she seemed personable and smart. I needed someone to teach so I could go out and help people with interpreting and residencias etc, so I took her on.

Well, it all started well, though some students said they couldn´t understand her English explanations very well. Fair enough. I asked her to speak more slowly to them.

Then strange reports were coming back from the students, very mixed feedback. One day it would be:

-"Consuelo is a terrible teacher, I didn´t understand anything".

The next day:

- "Just had a brilliant class with Consuelo, it was fab"- sometimes from the same person!!!

I know that you can´t please all the people all the time, so we persevered.

Then she started not always turning up for classes- We would have 6 students waiting and no teacher.

My other teacher Ester sometime stepped in or I would have to come back from wherever I was with clients and take the class.

I sat her down for a talk. She became very emotional and told me her father was dying of cancer. This especially struck a chord with me as very recently at the time my own father had died suddenly and I was devastated.

We talked at length, and I gave her many more chances than she ever deserved.

Looking back, I think this is the worst thing she did, using her father´s illness (I still don´t know if it was real or not) to excuse her behaviour.

A couple of months passed and things didn´t improve. It all came to a head one Friday afternoon when she didn´t turn up (again) leaving a full group of students stranded. I was miles away and couldn´t get back. We tried and tried to get through to her to no avail.

When I finally got through, there was no apology, no reason given, she sounded like she had just woken up. So, I regretfully informed her I would not be needing her services anymore.

It was like a bomb had gone off...

She began to scream, and I mean scream, that she would report me to the Spanish authorities.... There were laws in this country... I could not do it.... She would see me go to prison... How dare I.... I was just a foreigner and would not get away with it etc etc...

Over the weekend I was bombarded with similar calls, including one from her female "solicitor" (strange that they were working on a Sunday) threatening me with legal action.

The only good thing about this was it all made me feel less guilty about letting her go.

The following Monday I went into work and explained to the other teacher what had happened.

She said " Thank God you finally got rid of her, she is a cocaine addict but I didn´t like to tell you"

Great. Thanks for that.

Looking back, it all makes sense. The mood swings, the good days, the bad days.

Most teachers are happy with alcohol, I had to pick the one that was a cocaine addict.

Consuelo went on to open an Academy herself with her English boyfriend who interestingly enough had been the husband of one of my students.

Small world.

They had begun an affair while she was teaching him Spanish (before she worked at my school) and he had left his wife devastated for her.

Needless to say, the school didn´t last long.

CHAPTER 38- THE RECEPTIONIST/ LA RECEPCIONISTA

I always find it ironic that here in the expat community in Spain there are so many people looking for work, but when you need someone to do a job, good people are practically impossible to find.

The wages are low of course which doesn´t help.

I have lived in Spain for 23 years and it seems to me wages have never gone up, in fact maybe have gone down.

"La crisis" (the recession) and lately Covid have stunted economic growth.

Contracts are few and far between as it is so expensive in Spain to put your staff on contract, so few small businesses do it.

It is quite depressing when you advertise for work as you receive hundreds of applications, few of which are appropriate.

The first problem are people who have recently arrived in Spain. They have high UK - like wage expectations, (or wherever their country is) and they have not realised yet they will never be met.

If they are, they will be expected to work practically 24 hours and sweat blood, especially if there is a contract on offer as well. Sometimes they will be lucky to get paid what they are promised at all and may find out the contract they thought they were on in fact doesn´t exist.

My experiences of working for other people I will leave to other posts. But basically, bad experiences working for other people in Spain is the reason a lot of us work for ourselves.

If you are going to be insecure anyway you may as well be insecure working for yourself.

When Judy came along for an interview for a part time receptionist she was one of these.

She had recently left her job working for a big and quite prestigious company in the UK and relocated to Spain. I should have been prepared because if she mentioned this company once she mentioned it a thousand times, so much so that a student who was there at her interview actually messaged me later to say:

-"It takes a bullshittter to know one and I am one so I can see clearly that she is too".

I gave her the benefit of the doubt as I thought she was probably trying to impress, and she seemed to have a cheery personality and be very willing to please.

Another clue I should have noticed however was that she seemed to have brought lots of things from this company with her, stationery etc. Anyway, she seemed like the best of a not so brilliant bunch and she began work.

I am a very small business with a fluctuating income, even without Covid. Sometimes we are very busy, other times not so much. The job is varied, a little bit of anything that basically makes my life easier, and Judy was aware of and agreed to this from the start.

Some receptionists like the variance as I think it means the job is not boring, but maybe it wouldn´t suit everyone.

This is always made clear from the start, as it was to Judy, and she agreed enthusiastically. I did come to realise however her favourite part was sitting at her desk on the computer.

In my experience people agree to everything in the beginning then try to change the parameters as they go along to suit themselves and make the job about them rather than you. Judy was one of those.

She "friended" nearly all the students on Facebook.

She started taking a register of attendance even though that was something I did anyway.

She was permanently glued to her phone.

In my opinion I don´t feel I should have to tell a woman of over 40 that this is not acceptable at work. She only worked part time, so she had plenty of time outside work to sort out her personal life.

However, in other things she was good, no one is perfect, so I turned a blind eye to a lot of things in the beginning.

As time went on, she started asking for more hours. She said that she liked the job but needed more hours. I tried my best to find them for her.

Sometimes it is easier than others, depending on the time of year and how busy we are. After a while it became a constant strain so I had to admit I could only guarantee the part time hours she agreed to in the beginning, and I understood if she needed to look for a full-time job.

She said she would have to, but she would give me plenty of notice should she find one.

Time passed and I gave her as many extra hours as possible.

I constantly asked her if she had enough to do there is always something to do if you run out of work just let me know.

Yes, she agreed.

Another little irk I had was that she was always late. She did travel a long way, which was a concern I expressed at the beginning, but of course she said it wouldn´t be a problem.

The classes start at 9 and I wanted her to be here when the students arrived, so I even started paying her from 8.45 to make sure she was there on time.

Otherwise she would always arrive at gone 9.

This sort of boiled over one day when I had to be somewhere and waited until 8.50- no sign- and came out to find her sat in her car texting. I was a little miffed.

The worst thing however was the day one of my (then Skype-now Zoom) students had to leave the class briefly as someone arrived at their house.

It turned out to be longer than they thought so I was amusing myself on the computer. The computer I use for Skype is the one Judy normally used.

So I clicked into the "history"

Very interesting-

Weeks of visits to various sites:

Latest on X-Factor, Facebook, Google news, Colleen Rooney bust up, houses for sale. job applications, various entries to her personal Gmail account etc.

On one day there were 22 visits to her Google email account alone.

I was very hurt, as I had tried my best to give Judy as many hours as possible and it seems she had used many of those hours for her personal life. I did not mind the job applications etc but in her own time.

If she had asked me to use the computer for an hour I would have agreed of course. But honesty is everything. That she had done this while telling me she had plenty of work to do to me was unforgivable.

Or if it had only been a couple of personal things in one day- but not the extent it was. She only worked 3 days a week, she had plenty of her own time to see what was happening in the X Factor.

When I challenged her, initially she was incredulous that I was challenging her. She said:

"Oh, ok, so I went on the computer in my lunch break, is that bad?"

I had to remind her that in fact yes, it was:

- "Er, you are paid straight through, you only work part time you do not get a lunch break"

I did not mind her taking 15 minutes to eat her lunch, but looking at your emails 22 times in her lunch break that she does not have?

Needless to say, we parted company.

I wish Judy well; she bought my books to learn Spanish and then immediately blocked me on Facebook and WhatsApp.

Presumably she has enough friends now with all the students she added.

She never did apologise; I think she thought she was "entitled" her actions. At the big company she had worked for before it would have gone unnoticed.

Luckily, I have had nice receptionists too :)

CHAPTER 39- I CAN SEE CLEARLY NOW- COVID DIARIES 3 PART 1

If you are a reader who also follows my YouTube channels, you may know that last year, (2020) on the very first weekend of the "confinamiento" in Spain due to Covid 19, in March, I had a little accident.

I was washing my hair in the shower (one of those showers that go into a bath) and I slipped on some conditioner. fell. and banged my eye on the side of the bath.

I banged it so hard I gave myself a lovely big black eye that can be seen clearly on the videos I made around that time. I actually think I broke my nose as I have a little dent next to the eye socket. I have never washed my hair in the shower since!!

I did not go to the doctors or the hospital although I am sure I had concussion.

Covid was rife, hospitals were full, and what would they do anyway?

The black eye faded, I survived, and as time went on, I practically forgot about it though as I say I was extra careful in the shower ever since.

Time went on, and in September classroom classes restarted and things started to get a little more back to normal. I spent a lot of time on the computer finishing off a few book projects and updating my Break the Language Barrier series.

My right eye started to feel a little tired, and I started to notice a slight blurriness of vision.

Being one of those people that is absolutely useless at going to the doctors, I put it down to eye strain and waited for it to improve, resting my eyes as often as possible.

It did not.

Increasingly I felt I was viewing the world from this eye through frosted glass, though luckily for me the vision in my other eye was very good so I could function perfectly well.

As Christmas approached, I gave up thinking it would improve and contacted my doctor who immediately made me an appointment with the eye specialist.

By now I was panicking as I suffer from high blood sugar which I was not controlling well, and I was starting to think maybe it related to this.

I also wondered about the bang I had given my eye, had I detached my retina or anything similar? As we know, Google is great in some ways but can also give you sleepless nights!!

I turned up for my appointment very concerned.

The young girl I saw on the first appointment was lovely though seemed about 12. A sure sign of old age when doctors and policemen start to look like children.

She started off by saying it was probably related to the fall, couldn´t be a cataract as they came on very slowly not so quickly, then on further investigation saw that, ah yes, it was a cataract in fact.

I was absolutely gobsmacked.

Moi? A cataract?

Only old people have cataracts.

Ah hang on, I will be 60 soon, how the hell did that happen?

The nice girl told me that trauma to the eye can in fact cause or accelerate a cataract, but the good news was it was easy to remove.

I was given another appointment where the cataract was confirmed, and the process began leading to an operation.

Google was quite reassuring in success rate of cataract surgery, so I duly went along for my blood test and cardiogram.

Apart from the fact that my blood sugar was wildly out of control (that´s another story- now controlled) I was fit to go from February and told to wait for the call for a Covid test to be followed shortly by an operation date.

In the meantime, Covid (are you as fed up as I am of that word?) had taken hold again here and we were again under restrictions, with hospitals full again.

A couple of months rolled by with no news, but to be honest it was not getting any worse and I had learned to live with it. As my other eye was fine it really didn´t affect my normal life and I wasn´t looking forward to the prospect of surgery as I am a complete wuss.

The more I started to contemplate the fact that I was going to actually have surgery on my **EYE** the more terrified I became.

Perhaps it would be better if they just forgot about me, what did I need two good eyes for when I was coping well one?

Eventually I did call to check that I was on the list as things started to open up again and was told yes, all good, wouldn´t be long.

Bloody brilliant.

By then Spain was getting on with the vaccine rollout, so I was happy to wait as in my eyes (pardon the pun) they had so many more important things to do.

I put the operation to the back of my mind and just got on with enjoying our new freedoms as restrictions lifted bit by bit.

Then last week, it all happened...

CHAPTER 40- I CAN SEE CLEARLY NOW- COVID DIARIES PART 3- PART 2

I had waited 3 months since having an ECG and blood test in preparation for my cataract surgery with no news of a date.

I was starting to think I had been forgotten.

Part of me was quite happy as I was simply dreading the thought of my eye being operated on.

Everything I had read on the subject was encouraging, cataract operations are routine surgery these days with a minimal risk of complications apparently.

However, it was not routine for me I was frankly terrified.

I did not want to be blind though.

I could see perfectly well out of the other eye but it occurred to me if anything went wrong with that one, I literally would not be able to see at all.

I rang up just to make sure I was still on the list, and was assured everything was in order and I would be notified in due course.

Spain was really getting into the Covid vaccination programme, and I was happy to wait as I could see that this was more important than my eye.

We were all so desperate to return to some kind of normality.

I sat back and thought I may have to wait until the summer.

Just as I was relaxing into this thought, a week later on the Tuesday the telephone rang, and I knew instantly is was the health service as they always ring from one of those really long numbers.

Thursday- blood test in local Health Centre

Monday- Covid test in local Health Centre

Wednesday- Operation at Torrevieja hospital at 14:30

I was fine at first, I just accepted my fate.

I knew I was lucky to be offered this operation to recover the sight in my right eye. Many people in the world suffer this problem and are not blessed with the fantastic Health Service we have here in Spain.

My nerves increased slightly when Saturday arrived with a text informing me that my 1st Covid vaccination was planned for Thursday, the day following the operation, at 8.33 in the morning. I did not want to miss it but was not sure if I would be able to have it so soon after a medical intervention.

I enquired on the Monday when I went for my Covid test and was assured- no problem.

My nerves began to build as Wednesday approached, but I genuinely was fine until the morning finally arrived.

I worked from 9:00 to 13:00 as normal, trying to keep busy to try to keep from overthinking. I told myself how lucky I was with both the op and the Covid jab, again something many people would love to have to feel safer.

I think it was the fear of the unknown, and that it was my EYE. I seriously considered calling it off many **times** during that day.

Finally, 1:45 rolled around and my friend Jane arrived to take me to the hospital.

She was the perfect person to take me, so calm but caring.

My nerves were mounting.

I made a tearful farewell to my dogs as if I would never see them again and off we went.

By the time we arrived and I was waiting to be called I was trembling with fear, but determined to go through with it and trying not to be a baby.

The last time I literally came so close to chickening out was as soon as I was called into the day surgery ward.

I was taken to a curtained off area with some lockers and told to strip off to my panties, remove all my jewellery and put on two robes for surgery.

This instruction stopped me in my tracks for two reasons-

One -(I know seems ridiculous now) but I think this was the first time I realised it was an OPERATION I was going to have.

I don´t know what I had imagined before then, something like sitting in a dentist chair while they did it, and I realised there and then it was going to be done in an OPERATING THEATRE

Two -(even more ridiculous) -Earlier on visiting the loo I had realised I had my knickers on inside out.

If you like me are from a working class Northern family your mum also might have had a superstition for everything as did mine.

No umbrellas up in the house, laughing in the morning crying in the evening, drop a knife on the floor meant a gentleman calling.

The list is endless.

One of the many superstitions I was brought up on is that if you put anything on the wrong way round, i.e. t shirt inside out or, in my particular case that day, knickers, it would be bad luck to change them the right way around before the end of the day.

Well, the last thing I needed on the day of an eye operation was bad luck, so when I had realised earlier they were inside out I had not changed them.

Now here I was being asked to strip off and all I could think was I had my knickers on inside out and how embarrassing. I knew this was the last chance I had to run as once I was in the theatre gowns it would not be possible to sneak out unobtrusively.

I am very proud to say that I held it together. I was flustered enough to emerge still wearing my sunglasses on the top of my head and was shaking so much I could not get my necklaces or earrings off, but the lovely nurse sorted all that out for me and that's when I did finally accept that I was going to go through with this.

I did relax a little.

I was in chair 2 of a row of chairs similar to dentist chairs.

In number 1 was an elderly Spanish guy who asked me:

-"¿Te van a operar la vista también?" – he asked.

(Are they going to operate on your sight also)

I confirmed that they were.

Out of all the patients that came and went I was by far the youngest, and it was quite nice to be the youngest for a change :)

Apart from the guy I mentioned from chair one, and one other lady who were Spanish, all the other patients were foreign. British, German or Swedish.

And, apart from me, not one of these foreigners spoke Spanish.

This led to some very entertaining scenes which helped with my nerves as they disappeared behind the curtains and reappeared in various stages of undress.

Either not taking off enough clothes or taking off everything much to the nurses´ dismay.

It was like a Carry On film with the poor nurses struggling to make them understand, even though there was a picture on the wall in the cubicle showing you how you should dress.

Still, I bet none of them had their knickers on inside out.

Finally, Juan from chair 1 was taken off to surgery in a wheelchair and I guessed I was next as I was in chair 2.

He was brought back 30 minutes later and seemed cheerful enough, and it was my turn to be whisked away.

I was pushed down the corridor in a wheelchair, up to the theatre, given oxygen and a mild sedative and somehow the right side of my face was frozen, but I can honestly say that I did not feel a thing.

During the operation, which took only 15 minutes from start to finish. was the first and only time that I did perhaps think that maybe it would be better if I did not understand Spanish.

Torrevieja is a training hospital, and the surgeon was explaining throughout to a presumed trainee what he was doing.

Most of the time it was fine but there were two moments of concern.

One when he said: "I am going to ..... (didn´t quite catch what) because if not I am worried that .... (Again didn´t quite catch what) might happen".

Then again when the student said in what sounded like total astonishment "Ah really? Is that what you do? I never imagined that".

He seemed incredulous and the surgeon had to reassure him that whatever it was, was indeed correct.

It was a very surreal experience as I "watched" the cataract be doubled and removed, then the new lens be inserted rather like an eclipse of the sun.

And as I say, the whole operation took probably 15 minutes. Then I was sat up, back in the wheelchair and back to the reception area, where little old Juan from chair number one had already gone.

A patch was put over my new bionic eye which I was told to leave on until morning

I was offered a “cafe con leche” (milky coffee) or zumo (juice)and some “galletas de Maria” (biscuits) which was like music to my ears, as I had last eaten at 8 am and it was now after 4 pm.

The "cafe con leche" tasted like nectar and the "galletas de Maria" like manna from heaven.

I was allowed to get dressed and was moved to another chair as more people came in for the same operation.

I was feeling so relieved.

I was trying to reassure the other people waiting as I´m sure they were as nervous as me.

There was an elderly Swedish gentleman who was so happy to speak to someone in English he started asking me questions as if I was the doctor-

Him- "Will I be able to take my usual medication tomorrow morning?"

Me- "Er, I don´t know"

Him- "How long will it be before I get my other eye done?"

Me- "Er, I´m not sure, best to ask the doctor as I don´t know", (funnily enough).

As I was waiting for my discharge papers another foreign woman came out of her bay naked twice, much to the mortification of the nurses.

I wondered how often they are subjected to exposure of flesh from people who don´t understand instructions. The nurses didn´t speak much English but they shouted in unison "no, put it on!!!" in very practised English, so I´m guessing quite often. :)

By 6:30 I was home, 4 strong vodkas and some pasta later I was in bed.

I slept well and was up at 6 a.m. to walk my dogs as I had my Covid jab the next morning.

I gingerly removed my eyepatch, reminded of Jack Nicholson and the Joker as I cautiously looked in the mirror.

I had this awful fear that I wouldn´t be able to see or that my eye would be a mess.

The total opposite, I could see almost perfectly and apart from what seemed to be a strange lens above the iris of my eye it just looked the same.

I thought at first it was a contact lens or something that had been put there to protect where the surgery had been done, but when I went for my check-up later that day the doctor told me it was an air bubble that had been created as a protection and it would dissipate over time.

So clever.

Off I went (again driven by my lovely friend Jane) to have my Covid jab.

I was so relieved to have the eye operation over with I did not even worry about or feel my jab, it was a walk in the park.

I like people-watching, and I was struck by how people react so differently to things.

Some people just look away, take the jab and don´t make a fuss.

Other people are so dramatic, screwing their eyes shut and wincing, coming out clutching their arm as if they have been shot.

I wanted to say:

-"Hey, you think this is bad, I just had an EYE operation!!"

I was cocky now and proud of myself, as if I had never nearly not gone through with it.

The next day I was back in class.

I am so grateful for the fantastic treatment I received and feel truly privileged and lucky to have been blessed with both a "new" eye and a vaccination against Covid 19.

I want to finish this story by sending out love respect and prayers to all the people out there of all ages facing bravely much worse medical challenges and interventions.

You are awesome and an inspiration to the rest of us who are not.

Especially to one of my nieces who is facing one such challenge tomorrow.

CHAPTER 41- MYSTIC VICKI

This last week I have been reminded of both how lovely most people are and how they try their hardest to learn Spanish. Also, of how great it feels when students enjoy the courses and see an improvement on their Spanish because of our classes.

Unfortunately, I have also been reminded of how difficult and disagreeable some people can be and unreasonable in their expectations.

We can only give people the tools for learning Spanish we cannot learn it for them or improve their lives or personalities unfortunately.

Last Saturday was the Conversation Saturday. One lady had booked in quite a while ago.

I thought she had studied Spanish with me many moons earlier, she said she knew enough Spanish to have a conversation. The day before the course she sent me a message asking for the address which I duly sent and told her there would be a pink van parked outside, and that we started at 10:00.

Saturday arrived, along with the other students and the Spanish speakers, but this lady did not arrive. So, we started without her. I went upstairs to work on the computer. 20 minutes later the doorbell rang, and it was her.

I looked out of the window, I did not want to open the door as my dogs were barking and I didn´t want them to run out and scare her. I told her through the window the classes were downstairs- and I could see immediately she was not happy.

An elderly lady, I worried she might have a problem going down the ramp:

-"Are you ok?" I asked

"I suppose so"- she barked, "How do I get in?"

"If you just go down and knock and the teacher will let you in- Would you like to come in this way instead?"

"No" she snapped.

2 minutes later I heard the door open downstairs, so I knew she had entered.

I carried on working upstairs and could hear a lot of talking going on so presumed that it was going well.

About 15 minutes later I heard the door open again and everyone calling "adiós" and "hasta luego".

I looked out of the window and the lady was walking off up the road.

One of the Spanish speakers came up to tell me what had happened.

Apparently, she had come in with a face like thunder ("con mala leche" as we say in Spanish), complaining that she had been walking around San Miguel for 30 minutes, that she had thought the course was in the restaurant, that she needed water and a chair.

Both those were there waiting for her, so she sat down and the Spanish speakers tried to reassure her by drawing her gently into the conversation.

-"¿Qué haces en Navidad? - What do you do at Christmas?"

-"No me gusta Navidad- I don´t like Christmas"

-"¿Tienes mascotas?- Do you have any pets?"

-"No me gustan las mascotas- I don´t like pets"

And more in that vein, short, irritated answers.

I mean, how dare you ask questions on a conversation course?

Finally, she snapped:

-"I have to go" and stood up and went to the door.

The teacher asked her:

-"Are you ok?"

-"YES"- she barked.

"Do you want me to call Vicki down?

-"NO"- she snarled---

To be honest it was a relief when she left, she had cast a dark shadow over the rest of the group who were having a great time before she arrived, and had an even better time after she left.

When we went for out lunch later Maria from the restaurant said she had been in there looking for me and she had pointed her in the right direction.

Why she went there in the first place? - I have no idea.

I had sent her the address and told her exactly where it was.

However, her leaving meant the course went smoothly and everyone enjoyed it so much.

I hope she is ok, but sometimes people are their own worst enemies.

You do not do a conversation course if you don´t want to speak and being "mayor"(older) is not an excuse for being "antipática" (nasty).

Ironically, on the Monday a few days later I saw a post on one of the “buy and sell” sites from someone asking for recommendations for Spanish classes.

This very same lady answered recommending her daughter who apparently does Spanish classes in 6 different bars!!

Now I am even more confused why she even booked on to our course.

You just could not make it up.

So that was Saturday.

Then on the Sunday I was already feeling nervous due to some new students who were starting Monday with whom there were already problems.

This couple had booked the last 2 spaces on the course starting that day.

Then a week earlier, the lady had messaged me to say that they had been over to check the location and there may be a problem.

Was there a window?

As she was claustrophobic.

Our classes are held in the under build of my house.

I said no, there wasn´t, but it was not a small pokey basement, it was large and spacious and light.

However, they could sit upstairs if they preferred, where there was plenty of natural light instead.

Oh no, she said, they wouldn´t want to be separate from the rest of the group.

Ah ok, well they would be separate anyway as people can´t sit together due to Covid?

But fine, they could sit right next to the door, and we could leave the door open then as it was coming to summer anyway...

Oh no, she said, she wouldn´t want to inconvenience the other students.

Ah ok.

In the end I promised we would find a solution one way or another.

I restrained then from saying that if claustrophobia was a real issue for you in my eyes it would be imperative that you looked into all this before booking.

She said that I should have told her before that the classes were held in a basement and that there was no window.

Although many years ago I dressed up as a gypsy fortune teller for a charity event, I am not really Mystic Vicki.

I do not see that I could not have known that this lady was claustrophobic before.

Not once in over 10 years of teaching here has this ever been an issue, and so why would I ask?

The terms and conditions of bookings stated quite clearly on the website are that monetary refunds are never given, though I always try to offer alternatives if someone cannot do a course for any reason.

This lady seemed to be insinuating that I should have asked first if she was claustrophobic for some unknown reason, and the reason I didn´t was some sinister one.

Anyway, they arrived for classes and predictably she did not even sit down and try.

She was "going already" according to her as soon as she walked in. We had positioned them next to the door and left the door open, but this was not good enough as she had to see the street "properly" whatever that means.

I absolutely have total sympathy for anyone who is claustrophobic, it is awful,

However, I just cannot imagine why you would book on to a course, or in fact anything without finding out first if the place was suitable for you.

If your claustrophobia was so bad surely you would always want to ensure wherever you were going was within your parameters of tolerance.

However, apparently it was all my fault as I should have known by osmosis that she was claustrophobic and let her know there was no window.

I should be "ashamed of myself" according to her and they had been advised to make a denuncia.

(Denounce me for not being psychic?)

Also, she was going to blacken my name on Facebook.

Well. I have had had worse threats and actually the nastier she became the less bad I felt about the whole situation and the more my sympathy dissipated.

I just wonder when it became my responsibility to work out if other people are claustrophobic or not?

Maybe I should add to my adverts- not for persons with claustrophobia?

I mean, is it me? I always try to put my students first and be as flexible as possible but being clairvoyant, I really cannot promise.

I still offered her the option of sitting upstairs or even joining in on Zoom, or converting to private classes, but no.

She was determined from the start to not be happy with whatever I offered.

Another happy customer :)

CHAPTER 41- I BELIEVE IN ANGELS/ CREO EN LOS ANGELITOS

Belief is a strange thing. If you truly believe in something, does it make it true? People have such different beliefs, and many people are truly convinced that their particular beliefs are the truth, especially as far as religion is concerned.

I am not a fan of religion, especially exclusive ones that declare themselves somehow "chosen" and more special than everyone else.

I watch a lot of true crime videos, and you can be certain that the killer will be the "God fearing, church going, family person" nine times out of ten.

However, I see the point of it. It can unite people and it can offer solace and comfort.

As long as it is a tolerant religion and not hypocritical I can respect it.

As long as I am not expected to blindly follow it.

I consider myself spiritual but not religious, and respectful of anyone else´s choices. Certain things have happened to me in life that have convinced me that a higher power exists, though I lose belief sometimes and have to remind myself.

This story is one such experience.

My mother suffered from vascular dementia. She had a series of strokes after the death of my father and became progressively worse.

One such time I set off to visit her, travelling to the UK by car so I could travel around and also as I hate flying. My son Jack was about 7 years old. it was just the 2 of us.

The journey there was a dream. No problems, we stayed overnight in a truck stop in Cahors France.

Me, Jack and about 50 French lorry drivers. I would definitely recommend these kinds of places.

Really good value and fantastic food. My experiences in France have never been particularly good to be honest, but this was one of the better ones.

On arrival at Dover we went first to Reading for the birthday party of a friend and had a great few days. We carried on to Manchester to visit my

Mum as she was in hospital. This too funnily enough was enjoyable, spending quite a lot of time with my Mum on her ward.

Jack was the darling of the other old ladies, helping a lady with only one arm and leg to open things and not batting an eyelid at some of the unladylike sitting positions of the others.

He helped me brush my Mum´s false teeth and wash her hair, and it was so sad when the few days were up.

Although my mum was away with the fairies by then, she did come back enough to say "I don´t want you to go" as I explained to her that we had to return to Spain.

This broke my heart as I knew I would never see her again, I just felt it. She was so frail and confused. I´m just glad we did get that time together.

Off we went, stopping overnight again at my friends in Reading, then back on to the Ferry to return to Spain from Calais.

We arrived in Calais with 120 euros in cash, my credit cards and mobile phone. I didn´t have much petrol and considered finding somewhere straight away, but figured as I was travelling on the toll roads there were bound to be plenty of them, right?

Wrong. Word of wisdom (may have changed now), but there were NO petrol stations for ages and ages. These were the days before Google. Now you could just Google the nearest one and come off the motorway, but I was too scared to do so then and either get lost or run out of petrol.

I took an executive decision and stopped at one of those SOS phones, to phone for help and not take the chance of running out far from a phone and have to walk with Jack to the phone.

My telephone was not working, I had no signal, must have been when roaming wasn´t so easy as it is now, and no telephone had Whatsapp or internet then. I can´t complain about the speed the guy arrived, he was there within ten minutes with a can of petrol.

120 euros- shit. An expensive tank of petrol.

Never mind, I would pay by card.

Card didn´t work- double shit.

During that trip France was like the Twilight Zone for me- nothing worked.

Phone, credit card, debit card.

I had 120 euros in cash, but that was ALL I had. And I was just beginning my journey really. I had to pay tolls, get more petrol, and pay for a stay over.

What could I do?

"Do you have another card?"- he asked.

I was about to say no, then I remembered I did have the card details of an ex-boyfriend of mine, but not the card.

This, like everything in my life, is a long story.

Basically, this was a guy I had had a relationship with many years before when I lived in Reading, but we were still in touch. He lived in Gibraltar.

Earlier that year he had invited Jack and I to stay with him in Seville for a couple of days and given me the card details to book the hotel.

To cut a long story short, it turned out that he had different views of that trip than I did, and I had left early after barricading him out of the room- we had not spoken since.

I gave the card details to the guy on the roadside, I had the card number expiry date and security code. I told him it was not my card and I didn´t have the card itself, he said no problem.

I think he was just glad to get paid and get home.

The relief when that payment processed was palpable for both of us.

I know my (ex) friend wouldn´t be happy but what else could I do at the time? I would make it right later.

So, we set off again. I was rushing a little as I wanted to get over the border to Spain before it got dark, and this had taken time. I planned to stop somewhere then, presuming my phone and card would start working again over the border.

An hour later the Traffic "Gendarmerie" pulled me over for speeding.

Triple shit.

Anyone of you who live in Spain and think the Guardia are tough they have nothing on these lot for nastiness. Maybe it was the language barrier as my French is not as good as it was before Spanish took over, but they were plain nasty.

I just think if you are dealing with a woman obviously upset with a seven-year-old boy in the car you could at least be a bit nicer no matter what nationality they were.

The fine was 120 euros and I had to pay it there and then in cash. I

tried to explain that that was literally **EVERYTHING** I had, and that my phone was not working, my cards were not working, and I would not have enough money to stay over anywhere or even get to Spain, where i was sure I could at least ring someone for help or my cards would work again.

They were not interested. I think their exact words in broken English were- "You no pay you stay here".

I think my hysterical crying did rub off a little bit, and they did eventually say "follow us".

I presume they were going to take us to the police station or something.

I could not face it, I had to get home I had work the day after next. I gave them the money and I set off again hoping I at least had enough petrol to get over the border to Spain, and travelling on the "A" roads instead of the motorway to avoid tolls.

I drove through the night. Jack slept through it all luckily.

I was getting more and more anxious.

Petrol was going down and down and I was getting tired, but I did not want to stop as I was scared.

It was the early hours of the morning.

I prayed.

Suddenly a service station loomed up. One of those quite big ones that you come across on roads where many people travel. I do not remember where I was at the time though it was not far from the border, but still in France.

I had to go to the toilet, so I woke Jack and in we went.

It was deserted and quite eerie. Just us and the person behind the counter, I don´t remember if it was a man or a woman.

It was a big service station and there were loads of loos, none occupied.

We went into one of maybe 30 choices.

I could have gone into any of those toilets, but I chose that one.

On the cistern looking at me was a small red Radley change purse.

Radley has a Scotty dog motif on the front.

In that purse was a 50 euro note and a couple of euros in change.

No cards, no ID, literally that was it.

That´s why I believe in angels.

I bought some petrol and continued over the border into Spain, where everything worked once more.

My phone, my cards, I have never felt so much relief as I arrived in my beloved adopted country.

That was the first time I knew Spain really was my home, and I am meant to be here for better or worse.

France- forget it.

CHAPTER 42- UNA SEMANA DE CAOS/ A WEEK OF CHAOS

Even as I write this title, I cannot believe that so many things have happened in such a short space of time.

The first and worst thing that happened was more than two weeks ago, when my lovely older brother Tony sadly died.

Although he had been ill with dementia for two years, being looked after in a care home, in the end it was still a shock as he had survived Covid during this time.

I think we thought he would go on forever.

Although he was not himself, he was at least there.

There was a comfort in picturing him sitting watching the tele with a cup of tea and phoning him every now and again for increasingly difficult conversations as the dementia worsened.

I had hoped to go and visit him for some time, but Covid restrictions put a stop to that.

As they were lifting, I was making vague plans to go next spring.

My brother Tony was an incredible person, the life and soul of EVERY party with a machine-gun laugh you could hear a mile away. His nickname at work had been “laughing gas”.

His loves and “raison de étre” were his family, Manchester City and music.

Dementia took all those away from him in the final years.

A cruel, cruel disease.

I hummed and hawed whether to go back for the funeral, I had hoped to go back to cuddle him not to bury him.

However really, I knew that I had to go and be with my family. I had not seen any of my family in person for 6 years.

We are a very large family. I have two brothers and two sisters, and many nieces, nephews, cousins, great nieces’ and great nephews.

I am the “baby” of the family, my parents having a 10-year gap between having children, so I am closer in age to my nieces and nephews than maybe is usual.

Unfortunately, my older sister Susan is also ill with dementia in a care home, the rest of us are getting a bit worried as my mother had dementia too. I am hoping that all these years of studying Spanish will save me- they say learning another language helps so get those Spanish books out!!!

One of her daughters Kimberly very kindly offered to put me up and so I booked my flight and was ready to go on Saturday the 23rd of October to return Friday the 29th. On Saturday the 30th I had a “Conversation Saturday” booked.

On Friday the 22nd I was in class, half prepared for my trip the next day, but knowing I had the afternoon to finish off. I was flying at 10.30 the next morning so I knew it would be an early start.

At around 10 am it started to rain,- quite hard. 30 minutes later it was storming. I had one student in the classroom and one on Zoom, and another one arriving at 11.00 My Zoom student finished at 11 and the one arriving at 11 texted me to say she would come when the rain had abated a little.

Approximately 10 minutes later my student in the classroom said:

- "Oh look, do you think we should go upstairs?"- and pointed to the door.

What seemed to be a mini-Tsunami was flooding in under the door.

Within 10 minutes it was up to our knees. I can honestly say we were both terrified. We were shaking and my heart was beating so fast I thought I would have a heart attack. It just happened so fast and there was this sense of total powerlessness at the force of the water coming in. In the 18 years I have been teaching in my basement this has NEVER happened before.

We grabbed what we could and came up the stairs to the living room. Water was coming in from above also as I leave the door open to the sun terrace for my dogs. The other student arrived, and I thank God they were here to help me. The street was like a river, with chairs and tables floating down and cars submerged over their number plates.

It really was like a disaster movie. My students and I formed a chain gang, one of them actually wading through the water to get things and pass them up to the next girl, and then to me at the top, to salvage what we could.

Again, luckily for me, they were much younger and fitter than me, otherwise I really don t know what I would have done.

The rain slowly subsided, the students went home as it was now safe. The garage was so full of water at one point my dog was swimming around in it like a little shark.

I so nearly decided not to go to the UK. There were supposed to be classes Monday with my other teacher, but I did not have time to clear out the basement before leaving at 8 am the next morning. Not only that, physically I knew that I couldn´t.

All my clothes I had packed were wet from the water coming from the roof, I dried what I could and took the rest damp to dry once I arrived.

My students messaged me and volunteered to come in on Monday to clean the classroom, I will always be forever grateful for how kind people are.

So, I did go to Manchester the next morning.

I am a nervous flyer at the best of times. So many people on the flight not wearing masks did not help. The attitude from the Ryanair head steward was:

-" I ve been flying all through Covid and haven't caught it yet".

- Great.

Anyway, I arrived safely.

Although it was a sad occasion it was wonderful to see family and friends after all those years. Very emotional, laughing, crying, so many memories. Looking at photos, reading letters, a very intense time. I was so well looked after by my niece I cannot thank her enough.

The Monday after I arrived, I received a text purportedly from NHS test and trace saying I had been in contact with someone with Covid and had to isolate for 10 days.

Hmm. Obviously from that Ryanair flight where the steward had assured me I was safe. Maybe it was him that had tested positive?

Anyway, I turned my phone off and did a test daily for the rest of my time there.

I was always half expecting someone to turn up in a Hazmat suit and arrest me, but to be quite honest I was not going to isolate for 10 days, miss the funeral and also not be able to come back.

I tested negative every day and that had to do I'm afraid.

Wednesday, the day of the funeral arrived. We left early as I wanted to call into the care home where my brother had spent his final 2 years and thank the staff.

Alexander Lodge Care Home, Manchester.

I highly recommend this home.

I had not met the staff, but I had spoken to various of them several times when I had called by telephone.

Two lovely girls answered the door, and they knew who I was straight away. One of them was Spanish-speaking, and a subscriber to my You Tube channel.

Her name is Haymar-

Both girls were so nice and had lovely things to say about my brother. That he had a beautiful soul.

That was enough to start us off with tears and it set the tone for the whole day.

It had been pointless to put on our make-up that morning.

Haymar told me that she had many times put on the YouTube videos for Tony to watch and he had known who I was. I will be eternally grateful to her.

Earlier that morning my teacher had messaged me to say they had cleaned the classroom on Monday, but when they had come to class Wednesday to actually do classes the water had come in again.

I could not deal with it that day, I just had to say:

- "I'm sorry, but I cannot answer any more".

Then when we got into the car, my son messaged to say that his landlord, a very strange guy with some real issues, had rang the water board to have them cancel the contract and take the meter away.

He had no water.

This was the end result of a long saga that I cannot even begin to go into here, but which started with a leak behind the wall in the property that this fool seemed to think in some way was my son's fault.

He has threatened, insulted, taken illegal photos and videos. He has forged documents, forged signatures, and I have realised he has some severe issues, and it is just best not to engage with him but to let the police deal with it.

We have all his threats and insults recorded and a denuncia is pending.

An illegal landlord that has behaved illegally in every way.

I was miles away and on my way to my brother's funeral.

However, my friend very kindly went to bring my son home as he could not live without water.

Although this seemed a disaster at first this idiot actually did us an enormous favour. I could not have sorted everything when I returned without Jack´s help.

I believe in karma and sometimes things happen for a reason. This actually was the best thing that could have happened, so I feel enormous gratitude-

If you are reading this landlord- thank you so much.

The other thing that happened was my emails disappeared. If you have a website and you are thinking of changing your domain to another company- my advice would be- don´t do it!! I was not happy with the company I was using so decided to transfer the domain to another company.

My bad -though if they would have mentioned just once that this would mean losing my emails- I would not have done it.

My emails are with the same company but are paid separately so I just thought they would stay.

Apparently, I should have read the small print on the website. They were immediately cancelled and those emails I have used for over 15 years for both personal and business use. I am currently trying my best to recover them, and my website. I have certainly learnt my lesson.

So finally, I arrived home on the Friday to pretty much chaos, my son has a German Shepherd and I have 2 dogs and a cat (which I have now rehomed- Princess Tia does not like cats so that was an accident waiting to happen).

Again, the flight was a bit fraught as far as mask-wearing was concerned.

Note to self- do not fly from Manchester to Alicante on a Friday. I was joined on that flight by members of the "Benidorm Brigade" who all seemed to be Covidiots.

No wonder cases are so high in the UK.

The flight attendants seemed to be scared to tell them to put their masks on. The pilot made an announcement many times, even threatening arrest on arrival at the airport, but it made no difference

I was rewarded with some karma though, there, and then.

One charming (not) woman sitting directly behind me whose every other word began with "f" and ended with "k" knocked her full vodka and orange that had cost her eighteen pounds seventy-five pence all over herself.

I had not thought her language could be any more colourful but it turned out that it could.

I got up at 6 the following morning and cleaned out the classroom so we could go ahead with the Saturday Conversation class- we made it.

I think the students enjoyed it and that is all that matters. Gradually I am getting back to normal. whatever that is- Just dreading the next time it rains.

That´s it, for now.

If you are still here with me reading this, thank you so much for taking time out from your life to accompany me on this journey.

My blog is ongoing and can be found online. If you subscribe (which is free) you will receive notification of every new posting.

"Confessions of a Spanish Teacher"

https://wordpress.com/view/confessionsofaspanisheteacher.wordpress.com

If you are learning Spanish or English, you may find my YouTube channel useful.

Again, subscription is free, if you press "subscribe" and the notification bell you will always know when new videos are released.

If you want more content, you can join my Patreon channel.

For only three euros a month you can unlock all the extra content, and for 9 euros a month receive a free one-hour private Zoom class to ask me any questions you may have.

If you have enjoyed reading this book, please consider leaving me a review on Amazon, as this greatly helps with my sales.

I would love to hear any feedback, even (constructive) criticism, please let me know your thoughts by emailing vicki.riley@elprincipecentre.org.

Most importantly, please take care of yourselves in these difficult times.

Hasta pronto

Vicki xx

Printed in Great Britain
by Amazon

20769069R00188